THE
SUPREME
COURT

★

LANDMARK
DECISIONS

THE
SUPREME
COURT

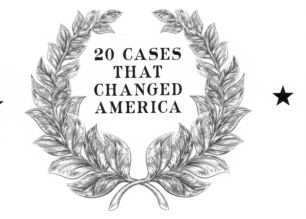

20 CASES THAT CHANGED AMERICA

LANDMARK
DECISIONS

– TONY MAURO –

FALL RIVER PRESS

New York

FALL RIVER PRESS

New York

An Imprint of Sterling Publishing Co., Inc.
1166 Avenue of the Americas
New York, NY 10036

ISBN 978-1-4351-6422-2

Distributed in Canada by Sterling Publishing Co., Inc.
c/o Canadian Manda Group, 664 Annette Street
Toronto, Ontario, Canada M6S 2C8
Distributed in the United Kingdom by
GMC Distribution Services
Castle Place, 166 High Street, Lewes, East Sussex,
England BN7 1XU
Distributed in Australia by NewSouth Books
45 Beach Street, Coogee, NSW 2034, Australia

For information about custom editions, special sales, and premium
and corporate purchases, please contact Sterling Special Sales at
800-805-5489 or specialsales@sterlingpublishing.com.

Manufactured in the United States of America

2 4 6 8 10 9 7 5 3 1

www.sterlingpublishing.com

Design by Shannon Nicole Plunkett

Art © Chris Gorgio/iStockphoto (laurel)
and © Pixaroma/Creative Market (symbol)

CONTENTS

PREFACE

The power and importance of the U.S. Supreme Court have never been clearer than in the early years of the twenty-first century. Since 2000, the court has decided the winner of a presidential election, declared an individual right to bear arms, rescued the biggest piece of domestic legislation in decades (also known as Obamacare), and cleared the path for same-sex couples to marry.

In most of those decisions, one side or the other argued that the Supreme Court was overstepping its authority—stealing power from other institutions or forces of our democracy. But the Supreme Court is a self-confident branch of government, not shy about taking on the most difficult issues facing the nation.

That bravado has become more obvious in part because of the dysfunctional relationship between the other branches. Congress and the president are constantly at odds with each other, and their ability to address tough issues is at an all-time low.

So it was perhaps inevitable that the Supreme Court would step into the breach. When the nation was thrown into weeks of uncertainty following the close vote of the 2000 presidential election, the court became the adult in the room and decided to end the recounts, handing the presidency to George W. Bush. "Get over it" was Justice Antonin Scalia's response whenever he was asked about it. To many the decision in *Bush v. Gore* seemed more political than legal. But it was also final, and the country moved on. As Justice Stephen Breyer has noted, it was a crisis that in other nations could have put military tanks in the streets to restore order. But in the United States the public peacefully accepted what the court had done.

Similarly, some felt it was not the Supreme Court's business to ratify the concept of same-sex marriage. The democratic process should work its will state by state, these voices urged, to allow same-sex marriage to grow more organically. But a majority of the Supreme Court felt the urgency of the matter and leapfrogged ahead of other institutions to get the job done. "The dynamic of our constitutional system is that individuals need not await legislative action before asserting a fundamental right," Justice Anthony Kennedy wrote for the court in *Obergefell v. Hodges*.

The Supreme Court did not start out as a muscular branch of government. It took the court until 1803 to assert itself as a coequal branch with this sentence in *Marbury v. Madison*: "It is emphatically the province and duty of the Judicial Department to say what the law is."

These cases, and some of the major decisions in between, are the focus of this book. In a meaningful way, because of the court's growing importance, they tell the narrative of American history.

The early growth of the national government and the American economy is captured in *Gibbons v. Ogden*. The curse of slavery dominates *Scott v.*

Sandford, and *Brown v. Board of Education* heralds a late effort to undo the damage. War powers were at stake in *Korematsu v. United States* and *Youngstown Sheet and Tube Co. v. Sawyer*. *Miranda v. Arizona* expanded the rights of suspected criminals, and a steady stream of cases elaborated on the guaranteed freedoms of the First Amendment. Hot-button issues from abortion (*Roe v. Wade*) to gun rights (*District of Columbia v. Heller*) to capital punishment (*Furman v. Georgia*) were fodder for some of the court's most controversial rulings.

Readers who are unfamiliar with some or all of these cases can be forgiven. As important as the Supreme Court is, it is the least-known branch of government. Fred Graham, who covered the court for CBS News, used to say that only the Vatican and the Central Intelligence Agency were less interested in press coverage than the Supreme Court. Of course, now the Pope has a Twitter account, and the CIA has a YouTube channel. The Supreme Court has neither, and is content to stay out of the public eye.

One consequence of the court's reticence is that few people know how it really operates. The justices agree to consider only a small fraction of the cases brought before them, and they do not explain why a given case is accepted or turned away. The court decides seventy or so cases per term, and each of the nine justices has four law clerks, sworn to secrecy, who assist them in deciding which cases to accept and in the writing of opinions. Oral arguments in each case are open to the public and represent the first time all nine justices are focusing jointly on the dispute. But after the oral arguments are over, the deliberations are completely private—until the justices issue their decisions weeks or months later. In that sense, the justices boast that the court is the most open branch of government because it explains the reasoning behind its rulings. The court does not allow cameras to record or broadcast its proceedings.

As the only unelected branch of government, the Supreme Court views itself as above and apart from the glare of the media and the political fray. But by increasing its muscle in deciding the most controversial disputes of our time, the court appears to be in the spotlight more now than it was in the twentieth century.

The Supreme Court became an election issue— at least fleetingly—during the presidential campaign of 2016. The death of conservative justice Antonin Scalia that February and the unprecedented, politically contentious delay over nominating his replacement underscored the influence of a single justice.

Appointing members of the high court is one of the most important duties a president has. President Gerald Ford once said he was "prepared to allow history's judgment of my term in office to rest" on a single act: his nomination of Justice John Paul Stevens to the Supreme Court. Ford left office in 1975, but Stevens cast a longer shadow, remaining on the Supreme Court until 2010.

Presidents come and go, but justices linger, exerting enormous power to influence the daily lives of all Americans.

MARBURY v. MADISON

- 1803 -

★   **JUDICIAL POWER**   ★

*For the first time, the Supreme Court declared
that it had the authority to strike down acts of
Congress as unconstitutional.*

In its early years of existence, the Supreme Court
was not a major player in governing the new
nation. It was not given a building of its own when
Washington, D.C., was built as the nation's capital,
instead occupying a small room in the Capitol.

More than anyone else, it was John Marshall,
chief justice from 1801 to 1835, who turned the
Supreme Court into a branch of government that
was equal in stature to the executive and legislative
branches. The dramatic change came in the context
of a seemingly ordinary case, *Marbury v. Madison*.

The case stemmed from a dispute over a group
of judges whose commissions were signed by Presi-

dent John Adams on the final night of his administration in 1801. Congress had authorized Adams to
appoint sixteen federal circuit judges and forty-two
justices of the peace as a parting gift of sorts before
Thomas Jefferson took office.

But John Marshall, whom Adams had appointed
as secretary of state in May 1800 and as chief justice in January 1801 (he served in both positions
simultaneously), did not deliver the commissions
to all of the appointed judges. After some political
maneuvering, William Marbury and three other
appointees who did not receive their commissions
asked the Supreme Court to issue a writ of manda-
mus ordering that their commissions be delivered.

By modern-day ethical standards, Marshall
would probably not have participated in a Supreme
Court case that had its roots in something he had
failed to do in his other government position. But
in December 1801 he ordered the Jefferson administration to respond to Marbury and the others
in the next session of the Court, which Congress
delayed until 1803.

When the case came before the court in 1803,
Marshall devised a seemingly contradictory way of
resolving the case. He said the so-called "midnight
judges" were entitled to their commissions. But
the ruling went on to state that Congress did not
have the power under the Constitution to give the
Supreme Court authority to issue a writ of manda-
mus to require that the commissions be delivered.

In that part of the ruling, Marshall said the federal law authorizing the high court to issue such

writs violated the Constitution. It was that aspect of the case that gave Marshall the opportunity to announce the court's broad power to strike down acts of Congress.

The ruling of the six-member court was 4–0, with the other two justices not participating.

In spite of the clear language in *Marbury,* the Supreme Court did not strike down another federal law until over fifty years later. Since the twentieth century, Supreme Court decisions overturning laws have become far more common, though justices say they do so only reluctantly because of the gravity of invalidating acts of Congress.

DECISION OF THE COURT
BY CHIEF JUSTICE JOHN MARSHALL

"The Constitution vests the whole judicial power of the United States in one Supreme Court, and such inferior courts as Congress shall, from time to time, ordain and establish. This power is expressly extended to all cases arising under the laws of the United States; and consequently, in some form, may be exercised over the present case, because the right claimed is given by a law of the United States. . . .

"If it had been intended to leave it in the discretion of the Legislature to apportion the judicial power between the Supreme and inferior courts according to the will of that body, it would certainly have been useless to have proceeded further than to have defined the judicial power and the tribunals in which it should be vested. The subsequent part of the section is mere surplusage—is entirely without meaning—if such is to be the construction. If Congress remains at liberty to give this court appellate jurisdiction where the Constitution has declared their jurisdiction shall be original, and original jurisdiction where the Constitution has declared it shall be appellate, the distribution of jurisdiction made in the Constitution, is form without substance. . . .

"The question whether an act repugnant to the Constitution can become the law of the land is a question deeply interesting to the United States, but, happily, not of an intricacy proportioned to its interest. It seems only necessary to recognise certain principles, supposed to have been long and well established, to decide it. . . .

". . . The Constitution is either a superior, paramount law, unchangeable by ordinary means, or it is on a level with ordinary legislative acts, and, like other acts, is alterable when the legislature shall please to alter it.

"If the former part of the alternative be true, then a legislative act contrary to the Constitution is not law; if the latter part be true, then written Constitutions are absurd attempts on the part of the people to limit a power in its own nature illimitable.

"Certainly all those who have framed written Constitutions contemplate them as forming the fundamental and paramount law of the nation, and consequently the theory of every such government must be that an act of the Legislature repugnant to the Constitution is void. . . .

"It is emphatically the province and duty of the Judicial Department to say what the law is. Those who apply the rule to particular cases must, of necessity, expound and interpret that rule. If two laws conflict with each other, the Courts must decide on the operation of each. . . .

"So, if a law be in opposition to the Constitution, if both the law and the Constitution apply to a particular case, so that the Court must either decide that case conformably to the law, disregarding the Constitution, or conformably to the Constitution, disregarding the law, the Court must determine which of these conflicting rules governs the case. This is of the very essence of judicial duty.

"If, then, the Courts are to regard the Constitution, and the Constitution is superior to any ordinary act of the Legislature, the Constitution, and not such ordinary act, must govern the case to which they both apply.

"Those, then, who controvert the principle that the Constitution is to be considered in court as a paramount law are reduced to the necessity of maintaining that courts must close their eyes on the Constitution, and see only the law.

"This doctrine would subvert the very foundation of all written Constitutions. It would declare that an act which, according to the principles and theory of our government, is entirely void, is yet, in practice, completely obligatory. . . .

"That it thus reduces to nothing what we have deemed the greatest improvement on political institutions—a written Constitution, would of itself be sufficient, in America where written Constitutions have been viewed with so much reverence, for rejecting the construction. But the peculiar expressions of the Constitution of the United States furnish additional arguments in favour of its rejection.

"The judicial power of the United States is extended to all cases arising under the Constitution."

★   ★   ★

GIBBONS v. OGDEN

- 1824 -

 FEDERAL POWER ★

*Broadening the authority of Congress, the
Supreme Court declared that under the Constitution, Congress has preeminent power over
the states in regulating commerce between the
states and with foreign countries.*

The Articles of Confederation, the first agree-
ment among the thirteen states of the nation
in 1776, gave the national government no
power to regulate commerce between states. Trade
wars and tariffs ensued, making it difficult to
establish a national economy.

With that in mind, the framers of the Constitution established in Article I, Section 8 that
"Congress shall have power to regulate commerce
with foreign nations, and among the several
States, and with the Indian tribes."

But the wording of the provision left confusion about the extent of the power given to Congress and what exactly constituted "commerce." The Supreme Court resolved the questions in *Gibbons v. Ogden*, giving a broad definition of congressional powers that helped the national economy to grow to the colossus that it is today.

The origin of the case illustrated the fact that states were still squabbling with each other over trade issues in spite of the Constitution's grant of commerce power to Congress. Robert Fulton, inventor of the steamboat, was able to obtain an exclusive license from New York for steam navigation within the state and in interstate waterways as well. They licensed Aaron Ogden to run a ferry between New York City and New Jersey. But Thomas Gibbons held a federal coastal license to operate boats in competing routes.

Their dispute reached the Supreme Court as the first major test of the Commerce Clause. By a 6–0 vote the court, led by Chief Justice John Marshall, agreed that "the power to regulate commerce extends to every species of commercial intercourse between the United States and foreign nations, and among the several States." That expansive view included navigation. The ruling allowed that states can regulate commerce entirely within their own boundaries, and said that states could still enact and enforce certain kinds of health and inspection laws that affect commerce. Justice William Johnson wrote a concurrence that gave an even more expansive interpretation of the commerce power.

The decision had the immediate impact of canceling Ogden's monopoly, but the importance of *Gibbons v. Ogden* has grown ever since. Congress has invoked its commerce power in a broad range of areas ranging from antitrust regulations to the prohibition of marijuana sales. In the 1964 case *Heart of Atlanta Motel v. United States*, the Supreme Court agreed that the Commerce Clause justified the provision of the Civil Rights Act that barred racial discrimination in public accommodations, because interstate commerce was involved.

DECISION OF THE COURT
BY CHIEF JUSTICE JOHN MARSHALL

"The subject to which the power is next applied is to commerce 'among the several States.' The word 'among' means intermingled with. A thing which is among others is intermingled with them. Commerce among the States cannot stop at the external boundary line of each State, but may be introduced into the interior.

"It is not intended to say that these words comprehend that commerce which is completely internal, which is carried on between man and man in a State, or between different parts of the same State, and which does not extend to or affect other States. Such a power would be inconvenient, and is certainly unnecessary.

"Comprehensive as the word 'among' is, it may very properly be restricted to that commerce which concerns more States than one. The phrase is not one which would probably have been selected to indicate the completely interior traffic of a State, because it is not an apt phrase for that purpose, and the enumeration of the particular classes of commerce to which the power was to be extended would not have been made had the intention been to extend the power to every description. The enumeration presupposes something not enumerated, and that something, if we regard the language or the subject of the sentence, must be the exclusively internal commerce of a State. The genius and character of the whole government seem to be that its action is to be applied to all the external concerns of the nation, and to those internal concerns which affect the States generally, but not to those which are completely within a particular State, which do not affect other States, and with which it is not necessary to interfere for the purpose of executing some of the general powers of the government. The completely internal commerce of a State, then, may be considered as reserved for the State itself.

"But, in regulating commerce with foreign nations, the power of Congress does not stop at the jurisdictional lines of the several States. It would be a very useless power if it could not pass those lines. The commerce of the United States with foreign nations is that of the whole United States. Every district has a right to participate in it. The deep streams which penetrate our country in every direction pass through the interior of almost every State in the Union, and furnish the means of exercising this right. If Congress has the power to regulate it, that power must be exercised whenever the subject exists. If it exists within the States, if a foreign voyage may commence or terminate at a port within a State, then the power of Congress may be exercised within a State. . . .

". . . [I]t has been contended that if a law passed by a State, in the exercise of its acknowledged sovereignty, comes into conflict with a law passed by Congress in pursuance of the Constitution, they affect the subject and each other like equal opposing powers.

"But the framers of our Constitution foresaw this state of things, and provided for it by declaring the supremacy not only of itself, but of the laws made in pursuance of it. The nullity of any act inconsistent with the Constitution is produced by the declaration that the Constitution is the supreme law. The appropriate application of that part of the clause which confers the same supremacy on laws and treaties is to such acts of the State Legislatures as do not transcend their powers, but, though enacted in the execution of acknowledged State powers, interfere with, or are contrary to, the laws of Congress made in pursuance of the Constitution or some treaty made under the authority of the United States. In every such case, the act of Congress or the treaty is supreme, and the law of the State, though enacted in the exercise of powers not controverted, must yield to it. . . .

"We are now arrived at the inquiry—What is this power?

"It is the power to regulate, that is, to prescribe the rule by which commerce is to be governed. This power, like all others vested in Congress, is complete in itself, may be exercised to its utmost extent, and acknowledges no limitations other than are prescribed in the Constitution. These are expressed in plain terms, and do not affect the questions which arise in this case, or which have been discussed at the bar. If, as has always been understood, the sovereignty of Congress, though limited to specified objects, is plenary as to those objects, the power over commerce with foreign nations, and among the several States, is vested in Congress as absolutely as it would be in a single government, having in its Constitution the same restrictions on the exercise of the power as are found in the Constitution of the United States. The wisdom and the discretion of Congress, their identity with the people, and the influence which their constituents possess at elections are, in this, as in many other instances, as that, for example, of declaring war, the sole restraints on which they have relied, to secure them from its abuse. They are the restraints on which the people must often rely solely, in all representative governments.

"The power of Congress, then, comprehends navigation, within the limits of every State in the Union, so far as that navigation may be in any manner connected with 'commerce with foreign nations, or among the several States, or with the Indian tribes.' It may, of consequence, pass the jurisdictional line of New York and act upon the very waters to which the prohibition now under consideration applies."

CONCURRING OPINION
BY JUSTICE WILLIAM JOHNSON

"The judgment entered by the Court in this cause, has my entire approbation, but, having adopted my conclusions on views of the subject materially different from those of my brethren, I feel it incumbent on me to exhibit those views. I have also another inducement: in questions of great importance and great delicacy, I feel my duty to the public best discharged by an effort to maintain my opinions in my own way.

"In attempts to construe the Constitution, I have never found much benefit resulting from the inquiry whether the whole or any part of it is to be construed strictly or literally. The simple, classical, precise, yet comprehensive language in which it is couched leaves, at most, but very little latitude for construction, and when its intent and meaning is discovered, nothing remains but to execute the will of those who made it in the best manner to effect the purposes intended. The great and paramount purpose was to unite this mass of wealth and power, for the protection of the humblest individual, his rights, civil and political, his interests and prosperity, are the sole end; the rest are nothing but the means. But the principal of those means, one so essential as to approach nearer the characteristics of an end, was the independence and harmony of the States that they may the better subserve the purposes of cherishing and protecting the respective families of this great republic. . . .

"The 'power to regulate commerce' here meant to be granted was that power to regulate commerce which previously existed in the States. But what was that power? The States were unquestionably supreme, and each possessed that power over commerce which is acknowledged to reside in every sovereign State. The definition and limits of that power are to be sought among the features of international law, and, as it was not only admitted but insisted on by both parties in argument that, 'unaffected by a state of war, by treaties, or by municipal regulations, all commerce among independent States was legitimate,' there is no necessity to appeal to the oracles of the *jus commune* for the correctness of that doctrine. The law of nations, regarding man as a social animal, pronounces all commerce legitimate in a state of peace until prohibited by positive law. The power of a sovereign state over commerce therefore amounts to nothing more than a power to limit and restrain it at pleasure. And since the power to prescribe the limits to its freedom necessarily implies the power to determine what shall remain unrestrained, it follows that the power must be exclusive; it can reside but in one potentate, and hence the grant of this power carries with it the whole subject, leaving nothing for the State to act upon."

★　★　★

SCOTT v. SANDFORD

– 1857 –

★ **SLAVERY AND RACIAL** ★
DISCRIMINATION

In a decision that foreshadowed the Civil War, the Supreme Court ruled that former African-American slaves were not citizens of the United States and could not become citizens. It also ruled that Congress did not have the authority to prohibit slavery in the territories. As a result, the Missouri Compromise, which outlawed slavery in parts of the Louisiana Territory, was found unconstitutional.

Slavery was an intensely divisive issue before the Civil War—especially pertaining to the status of slavery in the new territories that became part of the United States. The new Republican Party worked to prevent the spread of slavery in these areas, but Congress did not resolve the issue. Eventually it fell to the Supreme Court to provide an answer. It did so in the case of Dred Scott, a native of Virginia who was sold as a slave to John Emerson, a St. Louis doctor.

Emerson took Scott along when he joined the military and brought him to various postings, including the Wisconsin Territory, where slavery was prohibited. While there, Scott married another slave, Harriet Robinson. During a tour in Louisiana, Emerson married Irene Sanford. When Emerson was transferred to Florida, his wife and the Scotts returned to St. Louis. Dr. Emerson died in 1843, but the Scotts continued to work for his widow and for her brother, John Sanford of New York.

Scott sued for his freedom in 1847, claiming that he and his wife had been emancipated in the Wisconsin Territory. The Missouri Supreme Court ruled that Scott was still a slave.

Scott's lawyers wanted to appeal the case to the U.S. Supreme Court, and the best way to do this was to present it as a dispute between citizens of different states. The lawyers picked John Sanford, who was his sister's agent in the litigation, as the defendant. For his part, Scott claimed he was a Missouri citizen. The case became known as *Scott v. Sandford* because Sanford's name was misspelled in the records.

The Supreme Court heard arguments in the case twice in 1856. With five of the nine justices coming from slaveholding families, Scott's chances of victory were slim. Chief Justice Taney was a Marylander already on record in support of slavery.

The Supreme Court issued its ruling against Scott in 1857. Chief Justice Roger Taney wrote for the court. Justices James Wayne, John Catron, Peter Daniel, Samuel Nelson, Robert C. Grier, and John Campbell joined the majority. Justices John McLean and Benjamin Curtis dissented. All nine justices wrote separate opinions.

Taney made his views clear when he wrote that even though the Declaration of Independence declares that "all men are created equal," it was "too clear for dispute, that the enslaved African race were not intended to be included."

The Court had declared slavery to be a national institution that Congress could not prohibit in the territories. Reaction to the decision was swift. Abolitionist Horace Greeley's *New-York Tribune* said the decision "is entitled to just so much moral weight as would be the judgment of those congregated in any Washington bar room." A Georgia newspaper countered that "southern opinion on the subject of southern slavery is now the supreme law of the land."

Historians generally view the Dred Scott decision as one of the court's most embarrassing rulings. Decades later, Chief Justice Charles Evans Hughes described it as the court's greatest "self-inflicted wound." While it may not have caused the Civil War to break out, it was probably a contributing factor.

It took a constitutional amendment—the Thirteenth—to undo the damage of *Scott v. Sandford* by abolishing slavery in 1865. But it had one lasting legacy. It is viewed as the first time a major federal law—the Missouri Compromise—was ruled unconstitutional.

DECISION OF THE COURT
BY CHIEF JUSTICE ROGER TANEY

"The question before us is whether the class of persons described in the plea in abatement compose a portion of this people, and are constituent members of this sovereignty? We think they are not, and that they are not included, and were not intended to be included, under the word 'citizens' in the Constitution, and can therefore claim none of the rights and privileges which that instrument provides for and secures to citizens of the United States. . . .

"In the opinion of the court, the legislation and histories of the times, and the language used in the Declaration of Independence, show that neither the class of persons who had been imported as slaves, nor their descendants, whether they had become free or not, were then acknowledged as a part of the people, nor intended to be included in the general words used in that memorable instrument.

". . . [T]he right of property in a slave is distinctly and expressly affirmed in the Constitution. The right to traffic in it, like an ordinary article of merchandise and property, was guaranteed to the citizens of the United States in every State that might desire it for twenty years. . . .

". . . [I]t is the opinion of the Court that the act of Congress which prohibited a citizen from holding and owning property of this kind in the territory of the United States north of the line therein mentioned is not warranted by the Constitution, and is therefore void; and that neither Dred Scott himself nor any of his family were made free by being carried into this territory, even if they had been carried there by the owner with the intention of becoming a permanent resident. . . .

"The question then arises, whether the provisions of the Constitution, in relation to the personal rights and privileges to which the citizen of a State should be entitled, embraced the negro African race, at that time in this country or who might afterwards be imported, who had then or should afterwards be made free in any State, and to put it in the power of a single State to make him a citizen of the United States and endue him with the full rights of citizenship in every other State without their consent? Does the Constitution of the United States act upon him whenever he shall be made free under the laws of a State, and raised there to the rank of a citizen, and immediately clothe him with all the privileges of a citizen in every other State, and in its own courts?

"The court thinks the affirmative of these propositions cannot be maintained. And if it cannot, the plaintiff in error could not be a citizen of the State of Missouri within the meaning of the Constitution of the United States, and, consequently, was not entitled to sue in its courts."

DISSENTING OPINION BY JUSTICE BENJAMIN CURTIS

"Slavery, being contrary to natural right, is created only by municipal law. This is not only plain in itself, and agreed by all writers on the subject, but is inferable from the Constitution and has been explicitly declared by this court."

DISSENTING OPINION BY JUSTICE JOHN MCLEAN

"Being born under our Constitution and laws, no naturalization is required, as one of foreign birth, to make him a citizen. The most general and appropriate definition of the term citizen is 'a freeman.' Being a freeman, and having his domicile in a State different from that of the defendant, he is a citizen within the act of Congress, and the courts of the Union are open to him."

CONCURRING OPINION BY JUSTICE JAMES WAYNE

"Concurring as I do entirely in the opinion of the court as it has been written and read by the Chief Justice—without any qualification of its reasoning or its conclusions—I shall neither read nor file an opinion of my own in this case, which I prepared when I supposed it might be necessary and proper for me to do so. . . .

"In doing this, the court neither sought nor made the case. It was brought to us in the course of that administration of the laws which Congress has enacted, for the review of cases from the Circuit Courts by the Supreme Court.

"In our action upon it, we have only discharged our duty as a distinct and efficient department of the Government, as the framers of the Constitution meant the judiciary to be and as the States of the Union and the people of those States intended it should be when they ratified the Constitution of the United States."

CONCURRING OPINION BY JUSTICE JOHN CAMPBELL

"I concur in the judgment pronounced by the Chief Justice, but the importance of the cause, the expectation and interest it has awakened, and the responsibility involved in its determination, induce me to file a separate opinion. . . .

". . . The claim of the plaintiff to freedom depends upon the effect to be given to his absence from Missouri, in company with his master, in Illinois and Minnesota, and this effect is to be ascertained by a reference to the laws of Missouri. For the trespass complained of was committed upon one claiming to be a freeman and a citizen, in that State, and who had been living for years under the dominion of its laws. And the rule is that whatever is a justification where the thing is done, must be a justification in the forum where the case is tried."

SEPARATE OPINION BY JUSTICE SAMUEL NELSON

"This question has been examined in the courts of several of the slaveholding States, and different opinions expressed and conclusions arrived at. We shall hereafter refer to some of them, and to the principles upon which they are founded. Our opinion is that the question is one which belongs to each State to decide for itself, either by its Legislature or courts of justice, and hence, in respect to the case before us, to the State of Missouri—a question exclusively of Missouri law, and which, when determined by that State, it is the duty of the Federal courts to follow it. In other words, except in cases where the power is restrained by the Constitution of the United States, the law of the State is supreme over the subject of slavery within its jurisdiction."

SEPARATE OPINION BY JUSTICE ROBERT GRIER

"I also concur with the opinion of the court as delivered by the Chief Justice that the act of Congress of 6th March, 1820, is unconstitutional and void and that, assuming the facts as stated in the opinion, the plaintiff cannot sue as a citizen of Missouri in the courts of the United States. But that the record shows a *prima facie* case of jurisdiction, requiring the court to decide all the questions properly arising in it, and as the decision of the pleas in bar shows that the plaintiff is a slave, and therefore not entitled to sue in a court of the United States, the form of the judgment is of little importance, for, whether the judgment be affirmed or dismissed for want of jurisdiction, it is justified by the decision of the court, and is the same in effect between the parties to the suit."

SEPARATE OPINION BY JUSTICE PETER DANIEL

"It may with truth be affirmed that since the establishment of the several communities now constituting the States of this Confederacy, there never has been submitted to any tribunal within its limits questions surpassing in importance those now claiming the consideration of this court. Indeed it is difficult to imagine, in connection with the systems of polity peculiar to the United States, a conjuncture of graver import than that must be, within which it is aimed to comprise and to control not only the faculties and practical operation appropriate to the American Confederacy as such, but also the rights and powers of its separate and independent members, with reference alike to their internal and domestic authority and interests and the relations they sustain to their confederates."

SEPARATE OPINION BY JUSTICE JOHN CATRON

"That Congress has no authority to pass laws and bind men's rights beyond the powers conferred by the Constitution is not open to controversy. But it is insisted that, by the Constitution, Congress has power to legislate for and govern the Territories of the United States, and that, by force of the power to govern, laws could be enacted prohibiting slavery in any portion of the Louisiana Territory, and, of course, to abolish slavery *in all* parts of it whilst it was or is governed as a Territory.

"My opinion is that Congress is vested with power to govern the Territories of the United States by force of the third section of the fourth article of the Constitution."

★ ★ ★

KOREMATSU v. UNITED STATES

- 1944 -

In a wartime endorsement of the power of the federal government, the Supreme Court ruled that the president and Congress had the authority to remove Japanese-Americans from their homes in areas on the West Coast near military installations.

After the December 1941 Japanese attack on the U.S. naval base at Pearl Harbor, Hawaii, anti-Japanese sentiment grew quickly in the United States. Rumors spread that Japanese-Americans on the West Coast were helping the Japanese to plan an attack on the U.S. mainland.

Like most wartime presidents, Franklin Roosevelt did not pause to consider legal ramifications before he took action to restrict the movements of those with Japanese ancestry near West Coast military facilities. It began with a curfew but grew to include the "exclusion" of thousands of people who were moved to relocation centers inland.

Fred Korematsu, born in California, was one of those relocated to what became known as internment centers. He had tried to enlist with the U.S. Army before the Pearl Harbor attack but was rejected for medical reasons. In May 1942 he was arrested for violating the evacuation order. The American Civil Liberties Union, seeking to challenge the internment program, recruited Korematsu to make a test case.

By the time Korematsu's case got to the Supreme Court, the justices had upheld the curfew policy and his prospects of winning seemed poor. The justices confined the scope of the case to the removal order, without passing on the constitutionality of the relocation centers.

But Korematsu lost nonetheless, with a majority of the court deferring to the assertions of the military that the evacuation was necessary in the face of "imminent danger" posed by those being removed from their homes.

Three justices dissented, sharply criticizing the majority. Justice Frank Murphy said the court's decision went "over 'the very brink of constitutional power' and . . . into the ugly abyss of racism."

The decision had little direct impact, as the threat of a Japanese invasion, if there ever was one, had greatly diminished by this point in the war. The relocation centers were soon closed.

But the Korematsu ruling, by approving the evacuation of U.S. citizens based on their race and heritage, is widely viewed as an embarrassment that tarnished the reputation of the Supreme Court. In the 1970s the former evacuees began campaigning for reparations to compensate for their loss of freedom during the war.

The U.S. government in 1988 formally apologized for its treatment of those who were moved to relocation centers, and the dwindling number of victims who were still alive received some compensation. President Bill Clinton in 1998 presented Korematsu with the Presidential Medal of Freedom, stating that he "deserves our respect and thanks for his patient pursuit to preserve the civil liberties we hold dear." Korematsu died in 2005 at the age of eighty-six.

DECISION OF THE COURT BY JUSTICE HUGO BLACK

"It should be noted, to begin with, that all legal restrictions which curtail the civil rights of a single racial group are immediately suspect. That is not to say that all such restrictions are unconstitutional. It is to say that courts must subject them to the most rigid scrutiny. Pressing public necessity may sometimes justify the existence of such restrictions; racial antagonism never can. . . .

". . . [W]e are unable to conclude that it was beyond the war power of Congress and the Executive to exclude those of Japanese ancestry from the West Coast war area at the time they did. True, exclusion from the area in which one's home is located is a far greater deprivation than constant confinement to the home from 8 p.m. to 6 a.m. Nothing short of apprehension by the proper military authorities of the gravest imminent danger to the public safety can constitutionally justify either. But exclusion from a threatened area, no less than curfew, has a definite and close relationship to the prevention of espionage and sabotage. The military authorities, charged with the primary responsibility of defending our shores, concluded that curfew provided inadequate protection and ordered exclusion. . . .

". . . Citizenship has its responsibilities as well as its privileges, and, in time of war, the burden is always heavier. Compulsory exclusion of large groups of citizens from their homes, except under circumstances of direst emergency and peril, is inconsistent with our basic governmental institutions. But when, under conditions of modern warfare, our shores are threatened by hostile forces, the power to protect must be commensurate with the threatened danger. . . .

"It is said that we are dealing here with the case of imprisonment of a citizen in a concentration camp solely because of his ancestry, without evidence or inquiry concerning his loyalty and good disposition towards the United States. Our task would be simple, our duty clear, were this a case involving the imprisonment of a loyal citizen in a concentration camp because of racial prejudice. Regardless of the true nature of the assembly and relocation centers—and we deem it unjustifiable to call them concentration camps, with all the ugly connotations that term implies—we are dealing specifically with nothing but an exclusion order. To cast this case into outlines of racial prejudice, without reference to the real military dangers which were presented, merely confuses the issue.

"Korematsu was not excluded from the Military Area because of hostility to him or his race. He was excluded because we are at war with the Japanese Empire, because the properly constituted military authorities feared an invasion of our West Coast and felt constrained to take proper security measures, because they decided that the military urgency of the situation demanded that all citizens of Japanese ancestry be segregated from the West Coast temporarily, and finally, because Congress, reposing its confidence in this time of war in our military leaders—as inevitably it must—determined that they should have the power to do just this."

CONCURRING OPINION
BY JUSTICE FELIX FRANKFURTER

"The provisions of the Constitution which confer on the Congress and the President powers to enable this country to wage war are as much part of the Constitution as provisions looking to a nation at peace. And we have had recent occasion to quote approvingly the statement of former Chief Justice Hughes that the war power of the Government is 'the power to wage war successfully.' Therefore, the validity of action under the war power must be judged wholly in the context of war. That action is not to be stigmatized as lawless because like action in times of peace would be lawless. To talk about a military order that expresses an allowable judgment of war needs by those entrusted with the duty of conducting war as 'an unconstitutional order' is to suffuse a part of the Constitution with an atmosphere of unconstitutionality."

DISSENTING OPINION BY JUSTICE OWEN ROBERTS

"I dissent, because I think the indisputable facts exhibit a clear violation of Constitutional rights.

"This is not a case of keeping people off the streets at night, as was *Hirabayashi v. United States*, nor a case of temporary exclusion of a citizen from an area for his own safety or that of the community, nor a case of offering him an opportunity to go temporarily out of an area where his presence might cause danger to himself or to his fellows. On the contrary, it is the case of convicting a citizen as a punishment for not submitting to imprisonment in a concentration camp, based on his ancestry, and solely because of his ancestry, without evidence or inquiry concerning his loyalty and good disposition towards the United States. If this be a correct statement of the facts disclosed by this record, and facts of which we take judicial notice, I need hardly labor the conclusion that Constitutional rights have been violated."

DISSENTING OPINION BY JUSTICE FRANK MURPHY

"This exclusion of 'all persons of Japanese ancestry, both alien and non-alien,' from the Pacific Coast area on a plea of military necessity in the absence of martial law ought not to be approved. Such exclusion goes over 'the very brink of constitutional power,' and falls into the ugly abyss of racism.

"In dealing with matters relating to the prosecution and progress of a war, we must accord great respect and consideration to the judgments of the military authorities who are on the scene and who have full knowledge of the military facts. The scope of their discretion must, as a matter of necessity and common sense, be wide. And their judgments ought not to be overruled lightly by those whose training and duties ill-equip them to deal intelligently with matters so vital to the physical security of the nation.

"At the same time, however, it is essential that there be definite limits to military discretion, especially where martial law has not been declared. Individuals must not be left impoverished of their constitutional rights on a plea of military necessity that has neither substance nor support. Thus, like other claims conflicting with the asserted constitutional rights of the individual, the military claim must subject itself to the judicial process of having its reasonableness determined and its conflicts with other interests reconciled."

DISSENTING OPINION BY JUSTICE ROBERT JACKSON

"Korematsu was born on our soil, of parents born in Japan. The Constitution makes him a citizen of the United States by nativity, and a citizen of California by residence. No claim is made that he is not loyal to this country. There is no suggestion that, apart from the matter involved here, he is not law-abiding and well disposed. Korematsu, however, has been convicted of an act not commonly a crime. It consists merely of being present in the state whereof he is a citizen, near the place where he was born, and where all his life he has lived. . . .

"Now, if any fundamental assumption underlies our system, it is that guilt is personal and not inheritable. Even if all of one's antecedents had been convicted of treason, the Constitution forbids its penalties to be visited upon him, for it provides that 'no attainder of treason shall work corruption of blood, or forfeiture except during the life of the person attainted.' But here is an attempt to make an otherwise innocent act a crime merely because this prisoner is the son of parents as to whom he had no choice, and belongs to a race from which there is no way to resign. If Congress, in peacetime legislation, should enact such a criminal law, I should suppose this Court would refuse to enforce it.

"But the 'law' which this prisoner is convicted of disregarding is not found in an act of Congress, but in a military order. Neither the Act of Congress nor the Executive Order of the President, nor both together, would afford a basis for this conviction. It rests on the orders of General DeWitt. And it is said that, if the military commander had reasonable military grounds for promulgating the orders, they are constitutional, and become law, and the Court is required to enforce them. There are several reasons why I cannot subscribe to this doctrine.

"It would be impracticable and dangerous idealism to expect or insist that each specific military command in an area of probable operations will conform to conventional tests of constitutionality. When an area is so beset that it must be put under military control at all, the paramount consideration is that its measures be successful, rather than legal. The armed services must protect a society, not merely its Constitution. . . . But a commander, in temporarily focusing the life of a community on defense, is carrying out a military program; he is not making law in the sense the courts know the term. He issues orders, and they may have a certain authority as military commands, although they may be very bad as constitutional law. . . .

"Much is said of the danger to liberty from the Army program for deporting and detaining these citizens of Japanese extraction. But a judicial construction of the due process clause that will sustain this order is a far more subtle blow to liberty than the promulgation of the order itself. A military order, however unconstitutional, is not apt to last longer than the military emergency. Even during that period, a succeeding commander may revoke it all. But once a judicial opinion rationalizes such an order to show that it conforms to the Constitution, or rather rationalizes the Constitution to show that the Constitution sanctions such an order, the Court for all time has validated the principle of racial discrimination in criminal procedure and of transplanting American citizens. The principle then lies about like a loaded weapon, ready for the hand of any authority that can bring forward a plausible claim of an urgent need. Every repetition imbeds that principle more deeply in our law and thinking and expands it to new purposes. All who observe the work of courts are familiar with what Judge Cardozo described as 'the tendency of a principle to expand itself to the limit of its logic.' A military commander may overstep the bounds of constitutionality, and it is an incident. But if we review and approve, that passing incident becomes the doctrine of the Constitution. There it has a generative power of its own, and all that it creates will be in its own image. Nothing better illustrates this danger than does the Court's opinion in this case."

★   ★   ★

YOUNGSTOWN SHEET AND TUBE CO. v. SAWYER

- 1952 -

★ SEPARATION OF POWERS ★

In a decision that underscored the importance of the checks and balances that prevent any branch of government from becoming too powerful, the Supreme Court ruled that even in wartime the power of the president is limited by the U.S. Constitution and acts of Congress.

Congress did not declare war in the Korean conflict, but the U.S. economy geared up as if it were a war in order to produce the munitions and armored vehicles needed for U.S. troops.

When a labor dispute between the United Steelworkers of America and the steel industry threatened to shut down the nation's steel mills,

President Harry Truman moved quickly to stop the interruption in producing needed materials for the troops. After mediation efforts failed, he issued an executive order directing the Commerce Department to seize the mills so that necessary weapons could continue to be made. Responding to the order, the union canceled the strike, and U.S. flags were raised over the steel mills.

But the steel companies went to court, asserting that Truman's order exceeded his authority under the Constitution and federal law. Truman responded by claiming that his role as commander-in-chief justified the seizure.

The courts, mindful of the urgency of the matter, expedited the case and it reached the Supreme Court just over a month after the seizure order was imposed. Truman was confident of victory, in part because he had appointed four of the nine justices then sitting on the court.

But Truman was wrong. The court ruled 6–3 against the seizure order, finding that if neither the Constitution nor an act of Congress authorized the president's action, it could not be permitted. "The President's power, if any, to issue the order must stem either from an act of Congress or from the Constitution itself," Justice Hugo Black wrote.

But dissenters, led by Chief Justice Fred Vinson—a Truman appointee—said the result of the decision was that "the President is left powerless at the very moment when the need for action may be most pressing."

The decision was also a momentous assertion of the power of the court, and Truman's reaction to it proved the preeminence of the rule of law. Truman did not like the decision but he obeyed it, returning the steel mills to their owners. The steelworkers went on strike, and the strike was soon settled, with pay increases for the workers and price increases for the producers.

Youngstown was a pivotal case that is often invoked when there is a "power play" clash between branches of the national government. The war on terror in the post-9/11 period produced several such disputes. In *Hamdi v. Rumsfeld*, Justice Sandra Day O'Connor cited *Youngstown* when she wrote for the court that a state of war does not give presidents a "blank check" to violate constitutional principles.

DECISION OF THE COURT BY JUSTICE HUGO BLACK

"The President's power, if any, to issue the order must stem either from an act of Congress or from the Constitution itself. There is no statute that expressly authorizes the President to take possession of property as he did here. Nor is there any act of Congress to which our attention has been directed from which such a power can fairly be implied. Indeed, we do not understand the Government to rely on statutory authorization for this seizure. . . .

"It is clear that, if the President had authority to issue the order he did, it must be found in some provision of the Constitution. And it is not claimed that express constitutional language grants this power to the President. The contention is that presidential power should be implied from the aggregate of his powers under the Constitution. Particular reliance is placed on provisions in Article II which say that 'The executive Power shall be vested in a President . . .'; that 'he shall take Care that the Laws be faithfully executed,' and that he 'shall be Commander-in-Chief of the Army and Navy of the United States.'

"The order cannot properly be sustained as an exercise of the President's military power as Commander-in-Chief of the Armed Forces. The Government attempts to do so by citing a number of cases upholding broad powers in military commanders engaged in day-to-day fighting in a theater of war. Such cases need not concern us here. Even though 'theater of war' be an expanding concept, we cannot with faithfulness to our constitutional system hold that the Commander-in-Chief of the Armed Forces has the ultimate power as such to take possession of private property in order to keep labor disputes from stopping production. This is a job for the Nation's lawmakers, not for its military authorities.

"Nor can the seizure order be sustained because of the several constitutional provisions that grant executive power to the President. In the framework of our Constitution, the President's power to see that the laws are faithfully executed refutes the idea that he is to be a lawmaker. The Constitution limits his functions in the lawmaking process to the recommending of laws he thinks wise and the vetoing of laws he thinks bad. And the Constitution is neither silent nor equivocal about who shall make laws which the President is to execute. The first section of the first article says that 'All legislative Powers herein granted shall be vested in a Congress of the United States'. . . . After granting many powers to the Congress, Article I goes on to provide that Congress may 'make all Laws which shall be necessary and proper for carrying into Execution the foregoing Powers, and all other Powers vested by this Constitution in the Government of the United States, or in any Department or Officer thereof.'"

CONCURRING OPINION
BY JUSTICE FELIX FRANKFURTER

"The issue before us can be met, and therefore should be, without attempting to define the President's powers comprehensively. I shall not attempt to delineate what belongs to him by virtue of his office beyond the power even of Congress to contract; what authority belongs to him until Congress acts; what kind of problems may be dealt with either by the Congress or by the President or by both; what power must be exercised by the Congress and cannot be delegated to the President. It is as unprofitable to lump together in an undiscriminating hotch-potch past presidential actions claimed to be derived from occupancy of the office, as it is to conjure up hypothetical future cases. The judiciary may, as this case proves, have to intervene in determining where authority lies as between the democratic forces in our scheme of government. But, in doing so, we should be wary and humble. Such is the teaching of this Court's role in the history of the country. . . .

"It is not a pleasant judicial duty to find that the President has exceeded his powers and still less so when his purposes were dictated by concern for the Nation's well-being, in the assured conviction that he acted to avert danger. But it would stultify one's faith in our people to entertain even a momentary fear that the patriotism and the wisdom of the President and the Congress, as well as the long view of the immediate parties in interest, will not find ready accommodation for differences on matters which, however close to their concern and however intrinsically important, are overshadowed by the awesome issues which confront the world."

CONCURRING OPINION
BY JUSTICE WILLIAM O. DOUGLAS

"We pay a price for our system of checks and balances, for the distribution of power among the three branches of government. It is a price that today may seem exorbitant to many. Today, a kindly President uses the seizure power to effect a wage increase and to keep the steel furnaces in production. Yet tomorrow, another President might use the same power to prevent a wage increase, to curb trade unionists, to regiment labor as oppressively as industry thinks it has been regimented by this seizure."

CONCURRING OPINION
BY JUSTICE ROBERT JACKSON

"The actual art of governing under our Constitution does not, and cannot, conform to judicial definitions of the power of any of its branches based on isolated clauses, or even single Articles torn from context. While the Constitution diffuses power the better to secure liberty, it also contemplates that practice will integrate the dispersed powers into a workable government. It enjoins upon its branches separateness but interdependence, autonomy but reciprocity. Presidential powers are not fixed but fluctuate depending upon their disjunction or conjunction with those of Congress. . . .

"When the President acts pursuant to an express or implied authorization of Congress, his authority is at its maximum, for it includes all that he possesses in his own right plus all that Congress can delegate. . . . When the President acts in absence of either a congressional grant or denial of authority, he can only rely upon his own independent powers, but there is a zone of twilight in which he and Congress may have concurrent authority, or in which its distribution is uncertain. . . . When the President takes measures incompatible with the expressed or implied will of Congress, his power is at its lowest ebb, for then he can rely only upon his own constitutional powers minus any constitutional powers of Congress over the matter. . . .

"We should not use this occasion to circumscribe, much less to contract, the lawful role of the President as Commander-in-Chief. I should indulge the widest latitude of interpretation to sustain his exclusive function to command the instruments of national force, at least when turned against the outside world for the security of our society. But, when it is turned inward, not because of rebellion but because of a lawful economic struggle between industry and labor, it should have no such indulgence."

CONCURRING OPINION BY JUSTICE HAROLD BURTON

"Does the President, in such a situation, have inherent constitutional power to seize private property which makes congressional action in relation thereto unnecessary? We find no such power available to him under the present circumstances. The present situation is not comparable to that of an imminent invasion or threatened attack. We do not face the issue of what might be the President's constitutional power to meet such catastrophic situations. Nor is it claimed that the current seizure is in the nature of a military command addressed by the President, as Commander-in-Chief, to a mobilized nation waging, or imminently threatened with, total war.

"The controlling fact here is that Congress, within its constitutionally delegated power, has prescribed for the President specific procedures, exclusive of seizure, for his use in meeting the present type of emergency. Congress has reserved to itself the right to determine where and when to authorize the seizure of property in meeting such an emergency. Under these circumstances, the President's order of

April 8 invaded the jurisdiction of Congress. It violated the essence of the principle of the separation of governmental powers. Accordingly, the injunction against its effectiveness should be sustained."

CONCURRING OPINION BY JUSTICE TOM CLARK

"Prior to seizing the steel mills on April 8, the President had exhausted the mediation procedures of the Defense Production Act through the Wage Stabilization Board. Use of those procedures had failed to avert the impending crisis; however, it had resulted in a 99-day postponement of the strike. The Government argues that this accomplished more than the maximum 80-day waiting period possible under the sanctions of the Taft-Hartley Act, and therefore amounted to compliance with the substance of that Act. Even if one were to accept this somewhat hyperbolic conclusion, the hard fact remains that neither the Defense Production Act nor Taft-Hartley authorized the seizure challenged here, and the Government made no effort to comply with the procedures established by the Selective Service Act of 1948, a statute which expressly authorizes seizures when producers fail to supply necessary defense matériel."

DISSENTING OPINION BY CHIEF JUSTICE FRED VINSON

"Whatever the extent of Presidential power on more tranquil occasions, and whatever the right of the President to execute legislative programs as he sees fit without reporting the mode of execution to Congress, the single Presidential purpose disclosed on this record is to faithfully execute the laws by acting in an emergency to maintain the *status quo*, thereby preventing collapse of the legislative programs until Congress could act. . . .

"Seizure of plaintiffs' property is not a pleasant undertaking. Similarly unpleasant to a free country are the draft which disrupts the home and military procurement which causes economic dislocation and compels adoption of price controls, wage stabilization and allocation of materials. The President informed Congress that even a temporary Government operation of plaintiffs' properties was 'thoroughly distasteful' to him, but was necessary to prevent immediate paralysis of the mobilization program. Presidents have been in the past, and any man worthy of the Office should be in the future, free to take at least interim action necessary to execute legislative programs essential to survival of the Nation. A sturdy judiciary should not be swayed by the unpleasantness or unpopularity of necessary executive action, but must independently determine for itself whether the President was acting, as required by the Constitution, to 'take Care that the Laws be faithfully executed.'

"As the District Judge stated, this is no time for 'timorous' judicial action. But neither is this a time for timorous executive action. Faced with the duty of executing the defense programs which Congress had enacted and the disastrous effects that any stoppage in steel production would have on those programs, the President acted to preserve those programs by seizing the steel mills. There is no question that the possession was other than temporary in character, and subject to congressional direction—either approving, disapproving, or regulating the manner in which the mills were to be administered and returned to the owners. The President immediately informed Congress of his action, and clearly stated his intention to abide by the legislative will. No basis for claims of arbitrary action, unlimited powers, or dictatorial usurpation of congressional power appears from the facts of this case. On the contrary, judicial, legislative and executive precedents throughout our history demonstrate that, in this case, the President acted in full conformity with his duties under the Constitution. Accordingly, we would reverse the order of the District Court."

★　★　★

BROWN v. BOARD OF EDUCATION OF TOPEKA

- 1954 -

★   SCHOOL DESEGREGATION   ★

In a decision widely viewed as the most important of the twentieth century, the Supreme Court ruled unanimously that separate public schools for blacks and whites are inherently unequal. States that maintain racially segregated schools violate the Fourteenth Amendment's guarantee of equal protection of the laws, the court declared.

In spite of the constitutional amendments adopted after the Civil War to end slavery and guarantee equal treatment for all, true equality did not follow. The Supreme Court itself, in the 1896 decision *Plessy v. Ferguson*, approved separate facilities for blacks and whites on trains.

Segregated public schools were not just tolerated but required in seventeen states and the District of Columbia, relegating generations of black students to second-class educations.

But black soldiers returning home to America after World War II began to demand better treatment for their children. Civil rights leader Thurgood Marshall, later the Supreme Court's first black justice, began coordinating a legal assault on the *Plessy* precedent and on school segregation in particular.

In several states and the District of Columbia, African-American families began to challenge school segregation in the courts. Five separate lawsuits went before the Supreme Court, and the decision became known by the name of one of the lawsuits, *Brown v. Board of Education*. In that case Oliver Brown, acting on behalf of his daughter Linda, sued the school system in Topeka, Kansas. Linda Brown had to take a bus to attend an all-black school, even though she lived close to an all-white school.

The other cases, brought by African-Americans with similar experiences, originated in South Carolina, Virginia, Delaware, and the District of Columbia.

In the lower courts, the blacks seeking school equality lost in all but the Delaware case, where schools were ordered desegregated in 1952.

Arguing before the Supreme Court in December 1952, Thurgood Marshall asserted that school segregation was the result of "an inherent determination" to disadvantage former slaves and their families for as long as possible. As proof of the damage done by segregation, Marshall famously told the court about a study that asked black children to state which among four dolls they liked the best. A significant majority showed "an unmistakable preference" for the white dolls, Marshall said.

On the other side of the case, John W. Davis, a former presidential candidate and a noted Supreme Court advocate, said he doubted whether black families even wanted integration in their schools. Marshall emerged from the arguments worried about whether a majority of the court was prepared to order school desegregation.

In May 1953, the court ordered the case to be reargued in the fall—a signal that the court was divided on the issue of school segregation. But before the case was argued again, an unexpected development altered the outlook. In September 1953 Chief Justice Vinson suffered a heart attack and died. President Dwight Eisenhower used a recess appointment to name Governor Earl Warren of California to replace Vinson.

Warren quickly decided that the court should present a united front to the nation in favor of school desegregation. The other justices agreed, and what could have been a 5–4 vote turned into a unanimous one. Warren wrote the brief decision himself, using language that could be widely read and understood.

The decision swept aside centuries of segregation in favor of the democratic ideal of equality, though it put off for another day how—and how quickly—desegregation would take place. Reaction to the ruling was swift and negative in the South. Senator Harry Byrd of Virginia pledged "massive resistance." Most Southern members of Congress signed a "Southern Manifesto" denouncing the decision.

In May 1955 the court issued a second ruling known as *Brown II*, ordering local officials to desegregate schools with "all deliberate speed." But the court did not announce a deadline, and little progress was made.

After resistance to desegregation in Arkansas led President Eisenhower to send troops to Little Rock, the court issued a third ruling, *Cooper v. Aaron*, meant to speed the pace of desegregation.

But active resistance, as well as other factors including housing patterns, resulted in de facto segregation even though the court had prohibited it. The use of busing to integrate schools in spite of housing patterns was extremely controversial, and over time, federal judges curtailed busing and other desegregation strategies. No matter how powerful the *Brown* ruling was, realities on the ground have kept public schools separate and unequal even to this day.

On the sixtieth anniversary of the decision in 2014, Sherrilyn Ifill, president and director-counsel of the NAACP Legal Defense and Educational Fund, said, "*Brown* was no magic bullet for the problems of race and inequality that have plagued our nation since its beginning. We proudly celebrate *Brown* even as we recognize the ongoing, difficult challenges we face today not only in education, but in criminal justice, in economic opportunity and at the ballot box."

President Barack Obama, the nation's first African-American president, issued a proclamation on the anniversary that said in part, "*Brown v. Board of Education* shifted the legal and moral compass of our nation. . . . Yet the Supreme Court alone could not destroy segregation. . . . The hope and promise of *Brown* remains unfulfilled."

DECISION OF THE COURT
BY CHIEF JUSTICE EARL WARREN

"These cases come to us from the States of Kansas, South Carolina, Virginia, and Delaware. They are premised on different facts and different local conditions, but a common legal question justifies their consideration together in this consolidated opinion.

"In each of the cases, minors of the Negro race, through their legal representatives, seek the aid of the courts in obtaining admission to the public schools of their community on a nonsegregated basis. In each instance, they had been denied admission to schools attended by white children under laws requiring or permitting segregation according to race. This segregation was alleged to deprive the plaintiffs of the equal protection of the laws under the Fourteenth Amendment. In each of the cases other than the Delaware case, a three-judge federal district court denied relief to the plaintiffs on the so-called 'separate but equal' doctrine announced by this Court in *Plessy v. Ferguson*. Under that doctrine, equality of treatment is accorded when the races are provided substantially equal facilities, even though these facilities be separate. In the Delaware case, the Supreme Court of Delaware adhered to that doctrine, but ordered that the plaintiffs be admitted to the white schools because of their superiority to the Negro schools.

"The plaintiffs contend that segregated public schools are not 'equal' and cannot be made 'equal,' and that hence they are deprived of the equal protection of the laws.

"Because of the obvious importance of the question presented, the Court took jurisdiction. Argument was heard in the 1952 Term, and reargument was heard this Term on certain questions propounded by the Court. . . .

"Today, education is perhaps the most important function of state and local governments. Compulsory school attendance laws and the great expenditures for education both demonstrate our recognition of the importance of education to our democratic society. It is required in the performance of our most basic public responsibilities, even service in the armed forces. It is the very foundation of good citizenship. Today it is a principal instrument in awakening the child to cultural values, in preparing him for later professional training, and in helping him to adjust normally to his environment. In these days, it is doubtful that any child may reasonably be expected to succeed in life if he is denied the opportunity of an education. Such an opportunity, where the state has undertaken to provide it, is a right which must be made available to all on equal terms.

"We come then to the question presented: Does segregation of children in public schools solely on the basis of race, even though the physical facilities and other 'tangible' factors may be equal, deprive the children of the minority group of equal educational opportunities? We believe that it does. . . .

". . . To separate them from others of similar age and qualifications solely because of their race generates a feeling of inferiority as to their status in the community that may affect their hearts and minds in a way unlikely ever to be undone. The effect of this separation on their educational opportunities was well stated by a finding in the Kansas case by a court which nevertheless felt compelled to rule against the Negro plaintiffs: Segregation of white and colored children in public schools has a detrimental effect upon the colored children. The impact is greater when it has the sanction of the law, for the policy of separating the races is usually interpreted as denoting the inferiority of the negro group. A sense of inferiority affects the motivation of a child to learn. Segregation with the sanction of law, therefore, has a tendency to [retard] the educational and mental development of negro children and to deprive them of some of the benefits they would receive in a racial[ly] integrated school system. Whatever may have been the extent of psychological knowledge at the time of *Plessy v. Ferguson*, this finding is amply supported by modern authority. Any language in *Plessy v. Ferguson* contrary to this finding is rejected.

"We conclude that in the field of public education, the doctrine of 'separate but equal' has no place. Separate educational facilities are inherently unequal. Therefore, we hold that the plaintiffs and others similarly situated for whom the actions have been brought are, by reason of the segregation complained of, deprived of the equal protection of the laws guaranteed by the Fourteenth Amendment.

"Because these are class actions, because of the wide applicability of this decision, and because of the great variety of local conditions, the formulation of decrees in these cases presents problems of considerable complexity. On reargument, the consideration of appropriate relief was necessarily subordinated to the primary question—the constitutionality of segregation in public education. We have now announced that such segregation is a denial of the equal protection of the laws. In order that we may have the full assistance of the parties in formulating decrees, the cases will be restored to the docket, and the parties are requested to present further argument on Questions 4 and 5 previously propounded by the Court for the reargument this Term. The Attorney General of the United States is again invited to participate. The Attorneys General of the states requiring or permitting segregation in public education will also be permitted to appear as *amici curiae* upon request to do so by September 15, 1954, and submission of briefs by October 1, 1954."

* * *

SCHOOL DISTRICT OF ABINGTON TOWNSHIP v. SCHEMPP

– 1963 –

★ **PUBLIC SCHOOL PRAYER** ★

The First Amendment protection against government "establishment of religion" means that public schools may not require that Bible passages or the Lord's Prayer be recited at the beginning of the school day.

Before the 1960s, it was common for public schools to foster or allow religious expression in the classroom, such as a prayer or a Bible passage recited by teachers or students. In some places, that tradition continues to this day. It is not unheard of for school football teams to kneel in prayer before a game, or for graduation ceremonies to include references to a higher being.

But in the 1962 ruling *Engel v. Vitale*, the Supreme Court set a new course in interpreting the Establishment Clause of the First Amendment. No longer could public school officials require students to recite a state-sponsored prayer, even if objecting students were allowed to leave or not participate.

That decision caused an uproar among political figures and the public, still largely dominated by Christian beliefs. Some called for the impeachment of Chief Justice Earl Warren because of the ruling—just as some had urged his impeachment after *Brown v. Board of Education* in 1954.

In spite of the controversy, or possibly because of it, the court took up the issue again the next year by granting review in two cases, one from Pennsylvania and the other from Maryland.

In Pennsylvania, public school students were required by state law to recite at least ten Bible verses and the Lord's Prayer every school day. Students could be excused on written request by their parents. Abington Senior High School students Roger and Donna Schempp, who were Unitarians, objected to the Bible readings.

The Maryland case was brought by famed atheist Madalyn Murray, later known as Madalyn Murray O'Hair, and her son William. They objected to a similar law in Baltimore.

In both cases, lower courts found the laws to be a violation of the First Amendment bar against establishment of religion. The cases differed from *Engel v. Vitale* in that the prayer in *Engel* had been written and promulgated by the school district, whereas the disputed texts in the Pennsylvania and Maryland cases were widely available Bible passages and prayers.

By an 8–1 vote, the court reinforced the *Engel* decision by striking down the Pennsylvania and Maryland laws because they had the effect of advancing religion, contrary to the "neutrality" the First Amendment requires.

Justice Potter Stewart was the lone dissenter, arguing that the decision of the majority displayed hostility toward religion, not neutrality.

The decision was as controversial as *Engel* and still reverberates today in the debate over the separation of church and state. In subsequent Establishment Clause cases decided by the high court, justices have used a test that originated in the *Schempp* case, asking (1) whether the government's action has a secular or a religious purpose; (2) whether the primary effect of the government's action is to advance or endorse religion; and (3) whether the government's policy or practice fosters an excessive entanglement between government and religion.

Over time, the Supreme Court has grown more accommodating toward government-condoned religious expressions, at least in non-school settings. In the 2014 case *Town of Greece v. Galloway*, the court said that prayers offered at the beginning of a town board meeting were allowed under the First Amendment—in part because of the long tradition, going back to the time of the framing of the Constitution, of legislative prayer.

DECISION OF THE COURT
BY JUSTICE TOM CLARK

"It is true that religion has been closely identified with our history and government. As we said in *Engel v. Vitale,* 'The history of man is inseparable from the history of religion. . . . The fact that the Founding Fathers believed devotedly that there was a God and that the unalienable rights of man were rooted in Him is clearly evidenced in their writings, from the Mayflower Compact to the Constitution itself. . . .

"This is not to say, however, that religion has been so identified with our history and government that religious freedom is not likewise as strongly imbedded in our public and private life. Nothing but the most telling of personal experiences in religious persecution suffered by our forebears could have planted our belief in liberty of religious opinion any more deeply in our heritage. . . . This freedom to worship was indispensable in a country whose people came from the four quarters of the earth and brought with them a diversity of religious opinion. Today, authorities list 83 separate religious bodies, each with membership exceeding 50,000, existing among our people, as well as innumerable smaller groups. . . .

"The wholesome 'neutrality' of which this Court's cases speak thus stems from a recognition of the teachings of history that powerful sects or groups might bring about a fusion of governmental and religious functions or a concert or dependency of one upon the other to the end that official support of the State or Federal Government would be placed behind the tenets of one or of all orthodoxies. This the Establishment Clause prohibits. And a further reason for neutrality is found in the Free Exercise Clause, which recognizes the value of religious training, teaching and observance and, more particularly, the right of every person to freely choose his own course with reference thereto, free of any compulsion from the state. This the Free Exercise Clause guarantees.

"Thus, as we have seen, the two clauses may overlap. As we have indicated, the Establishment Clause has been directly considered by this Court eight times in the past score of years and, with only one Justice dissenting on the point, it has consistently held that the clause withdrew all legislative power respecting religious belief or the expression thereof. The test may be stated as follows: what are the purpose and the primary effect of the enactment? If either is the advancement or inhibition of religion, then the enactment exceeds the scope of legislative power as circumscribed by the Constitution. That is to say that, to withstand the strictures of the Establishment Clause, there must be a secular legislative purpose and a primary effect that neither advances nor inhibits religion. . . .

". . . [I]n both cases, the laws require religious exercises, and such exercises are being conducted in direct violation of the rights of the appellees and petitioners. Nor are these required exercises mitigated by the fact that individual students may absent themselves upon parental request, for that fact furnishes no defense to a claim of unconstitutionality under the Establishment Clause. Further, it is no defense to urge that the religious practices here may be relatively minor encroachments on the First Amendment. The breach of neutrality that is today a trickling stream may all too soon become a raging torrent and, in the words of Madison, 'it is proper to take alarm at the first experiment on our liberties'. . . .

"The place of religion in our society is an exalted one, achieved through a long tradition of reliance on the home, the church and the inviolable citadel of the individual heart and mind. We have come to recognize through bitter experience that it is not within the power of government to invade that citadel, whether its purpose or effect be to aid or oppose, to advance or retard. In the relationship between man and religion, the State is firmly committed to a position of neutrality. Though the application of that rule requires interpretation of a delicate sort, the rule itself is clearly and concisely stated in the words of the First Amendment."

CONCURRING OPINION
BY JUSTICE WILLIAM O. DOUGLAS

"Establishment of a religion can be achieved in several ways. The church and state can be one; the church may control the state, or the state may control the church; or the relationship may take one of several possible forms of a working arrangement between the two bodies. Under all of these arrangements, the church typically has a place in the state's budget, and church law usually governs such matters as baptism, marriage, divorce and separation, at least for its members and sometimes for the entire body politic. Education, too, is usually high on the priority list of church interests. In the past, schools were often made the exclusive responsibility of the church. . . .

"The vice of all such arrangements under the Establishment Clause is that the state is lending its assistance to a church's efforts to gain and keep adherents. Under the First Amendment, it is strictly a matter for the individual and his church as to what church he will belong to and how much support, in the way of belief, time, activity or money, he will give to it. . . .

"These regimes violate the Establishment Clause in two different ways. In each case, the State is conducting a religious exercise; and, as the Court holds, that cannot be done without violating the 'neutrality' required of the State by the balance of power between individual, church and state that has been struck by the First Amendment. But the Establishment Clause is not limited to precluding the State itself from conducting religious exercises. It also forbids the State to employ its facilities or funds in a way that gives any church, or all churches, greater strength in our society than it would have by relying on its members alone. Thus, the present regimes must fall under that clause for the additional reason that public funds, though small in amount, are being used to promote a religious exercise. Through the mechanism of the State, all of the people are being required to finance a religious exercise that only some of the people want and that violates the sensibilities of others."

CONCURRING OPINION
BY JUSTICE WILLIAM BRENNAN JR.

"The Court's historic duty to expound the meaning of the Constitution has encountered few issues more intricate or more demanding than that of the relationship between religion and the public schools. Since undoubtedly we are 'a religious people whose institutions presuppose a Supreme Being,' deep feelings are aroused when aspects of that relationship are claimed to violate the injunction of the First Amendment that government may make 'no law respecting an establishment of religion, or prohibiting the free exercise thereof '. . . . Americans regard the public schools as a most vital civic institution for the preservation of a democratic system of government. It is therefore understandable that the constitutional prohibitions encounter their severest test when they are sought to be applied in the school classroom. Nevertheless it is this Court's inescapable duty to declare whether exercises in the public schools of the States, such as those of Pennsylvania and Maryland questioned here, are involvements of religion in public institutions of a kind which offends the First and Fourteenth Amendments.

". . . I see no escape from the conclusion that the exercises called in question in these two cases violate the constitutional mandate. The reasons we gave only last Term in *Engel v. Vitale*, for finding in the New York Regents' prayer an impermissible establishment of religion, compel the same judgment of the practices at bar. The involvement of the secular with the religious is no less intimate here, and it is constitutionally irrelevant that the State has not composed the material for the inspirational exercises presently involved. It should be unnecessary to observe that our holding does not declare that the First Amendment manifests hostility to the practice or teaching of religion, but only applies prohibitions incorporated in the Bill of Rights in recognition of historic needs shared by Church and State alike. While it is my view that not every involvement of religion in public life is unconstitutional, I consider the exercises at bar a form of involvement which clearly violates the Establishment Clause."

CONCURRING OPINION
BY JUSTICE ARTHUR GOLDBERG

"The fullest realization of true religious liberty requires that government neither engage in nor compel religious practices, that it effect no favoritism among sects or between religion and nonreligion, and that it work deterrence of no religious belief. But devotion even to these simply stated objectives presents no easy course, for the unavoidable accommodations necessary to achieve the maximum enjoyment of each and all of them are often difficult of discernment. There is for me no simple and clear measure which by precise application can readily and invariably demark the permissible from the impermissible. . . .

"The practices here involved do not fall within any sensible or acceptable concept of compelled or permitted accommodation, and involve the state so significantly and directly in the realm of the sectarian as to give rise to those very divisive influences and inhibitions of freedom which both religion clauses of the First Amendment preclude. The state has ordained and has utilized its facilities to engage in unmistakably religious exercises—the devotional reading and recitation of the Holy Bible—in a manner having substantial and significant import and impact. That it has selected, rather than written, a particular devotional liturgy seems to me without constitutional import. The pervasive religiosity and direct governmental involvement inhering in the prescription of prayer and Bible reading in the public schools, during and as part of the curricular day, involving young impressionable children whose school attendance is statutorily compelled, and utilizing the prestige, power, and influence of school administration, staff, and authority, cannot realistically be termed simply accommodation, and must fall within the interdiction of the First Amendment."

DISSENTING OPINION
BY JUSTICE POTTER STEWART

"A refusal to permit religious exercises thus is seen not as the realization of state neutrality, but rather as the establishment of a religion of secularism, or, at the least, as government support of the beliefs of those who think that religious exercises should be conducted only in private.

"What seems to me to be of paramount importance, then, is recognition of the fact that the claim advanced here in favor of Bible reading is sufficiently substantial to make simple reference to the constitutional phrase 'establishment of religion' as inadequate an analysis of the cases before us as the ritualistic invocation of the nonconstitutional phrase 'separation of church and state.' What these cases compel, rather, is an analysis of just what the 'neutrality' is which is required by the interplay of the Establishment and Free Exercise Clauses of the First Amendment, as imbedded in the Fourteenth. . . .

"What our Constitution indispensably protects is the freedom of each of us, be he Jew or Agnostic, Christian or Atheist, Buddhist or Freethinker, to believe or disbelieve, to worship or not worship, to pray or keep silent, according to his own conscience, uncoerced and unrestrained by government. It is conceivable that these school boards, or even all school boards, might eventually find it impossible to administer a system of religious exercises during school hours in such a way as to meet this constitutional standard—in such a way as completely to free from any kind of official coercion those who do not affirmatively want to participate. But I think we must not assume that school boards so lack the qualities of inventiveness and good will as to make impossible the achievement of that goal."

★   ★   ★

NEW YORK TIMES CO.
v. SULLIVAN

- 1964 -

★   **FREEDOM OF THE PRESS**   ★

*To foster "uninhibited, robust, and wide-
open" debate that may inevitably include
utterance of falsehoods, the Supreme Court
ruled that the news media may not be successfully sued for libel by a public figure—unless
it can be shown that the news organization
acted with "actual malice" against the person.*

n spite of its sweeping embrace of freedom of speech
and of the press, the First Amendment did not at
first bring much protection for unpopular speakers and news organizations. The Sedition Act of 1798
made it a crime to write critically about government
officials. In a series of rulings in the mid-twentieth century, the Supreme Court ruled that libelous speech fell
outside the protection of the First Amendment.

As the civil rights movement grew, the white establishment of the South began to view the Northern press as enemies. By reporting on the mistreatment of blacks, the news media fueled nationwide demands for racial justice.

To strike back, Southern politicians and others began filing lawsuits against news organizations for defaming or libeling their officials and communities. The cost of legal fees and possible damage awards, the Southerners hoped, would discourage aggressive news coverage.

One such lawsuit was triggered by an advertisement—not a news story—in the *New York Times* in 1960. With the headline "Heed Their Rising Voices," a group of concerned citizens solicited support for the Reverend Martin Luther King Jr. Among other things, the ad mentioned police crackdowns on student civil rights demonstrators in Montgomery, Alabama.

Calling the ad "false and defamatory," Montgomery city commissioner L. B. Sullivan sued the *Times*—even though the ad did not mention him by name or title. The governor of Alabama and other officials also sued, seeking a total of $3 million in damages.

The newspaper fought back in Alabama courts, but a jury issued a verdict finding that Sullivan had been libeled, and awarded him $500,000. The Alabama Supreme Court upheld the verdict, asserting that "the First Amendment of the U.S. Constitution does not protect libelous publications."

When the case got to the U.S. Supreme Court, Justice William Brennan Jr. was able to persuade his colleagues to agree unanimously on a sweeping decision aimed at giving the news media "breathing space" to report on government officials—even inaccurately—without fear of intimidation by lawsuit unless the reporting was reckless or with "actual malice." Justices Hugo Black (joined by William O. Douglas) and Arthur Goldberg wrote separate concurrences, suggesting they would have given the press even more protection against libel suits.

By giving the press what has been described as "the right to be wrong," *Times v. Sullivan* has earned its place as the most important protection of press freedom in the court's history. For better or worse, the decision helped modern news organizations develop into the aggressive, sometimes raucous and obnoxious form of public discourse that is almost unique in the world.

More specific to the case before the court, historians also have viewed *Times v. Sullivan* as an important decision in the context of the civil rights movement. With the fear of litigation reduced, news organizations gave even more aggressive coverage to racial discrimination in the South, boosting the chances for legislation in Congress to address civil rights.

DECISION OF THE COURT
BY JUSTICE WILLIAM BRENNAN JR.

"The general proposition that freedom of expression upon public questions is secured by the First Amendment has long been settled by our decisions. The constitutional safeguard, we have said, 'was fashioned to assure unfettered interchange of ideas for the bringing about of political and social changes desired by the people.'

"The maintenance of the opportunity for free political discussion to the end that government may be responsive to the will of the people and that changes may be obtained by lawful means, an opportunity essential to the security of the Republic, is a fundamental principle of our constitutional system. . . . The First Amendment, said Judge Learned Hand, presupposes that right conclusions are more likely to be gathered out of a multitude of tongues than through any kind of authoritative selection. To many, this is, and always will be, folly, but we have staked upon it our all. . . .

". . . [We] consider this case against the background of a profound national commitment to the principle that debate on public issues should be uninhibited, robust, and wide-open, and that it may well include vehement, caustic, and sometimes unpleasantly sharp attacks on government and public officials. . . .

". . . The judgment awarded in this case—without the need for any proof of actual pecuniary loss—was one thousand times greater than the maximum fine provided by the Alabama criminal statute, and one hundred times greater than that provided by the Sedition Act. And since there is no double jeopardy limitation applicable to civil lawsuits, this is not the only judgment that may be awarded against petitioners for the same publication. Whether or not a newspaper can survive a succession of such judgments, the pall of fear and timidity imposed upon those who would give voice to public criticism is an atmosphere in which the First Amendment freedoms cannot survive. . . .

"A rule compelling the critic of official conduct to guarantee the truth of all his factual assertions—and to do so on pain of libel judgments virtually unlimited in amount—leads to a comparable 'self-censorship.' Allowance of the defense of truth, with the burden of proving it on the defendant, does not mean that only false speech will be deterred. Even courts accepting this defense as an adequate safeguard have recognized the difficulties of adducing legal proofs that the alleged libel was true in all its factual particulars. Under such a rule, would-be critics of official conduct may be deterred from voicing their criticism, even though it is believed to be true and even though it is, in fact, true, because of doubt whether it can be proved in court or fear of the expense of having to do so. They tend to make only statements which 'steer far wider of the unlawful zone.' The rule thus dampens the vigor and limits the variety of public debate. It is inconsistent with the First and Fourteenth Amendments. The constitutional guarantees require, we think, a federal rule that prohibits a public official from recovering damages for a defamatory falsehood relating to his official conduct unless he proves that the statement was made with 'actual malice'—that is, with knowledge that it was false or with reckless disregard of whether it was false or not. . . .

"We hold today that the Constitution delimits a State's power to award damages for libel in actions brought by public officials against critics of their official conduct. Since this is such an action, the rule requiring proof of actual malice is applicable. While Alabama law apparently requires proof of actual malice for an award of punitive damages, where general damages are concerned malice is 'presumed.' Such a presumption is inconsistent with the federal rule. . . .

". . . For good reason, no court of last resort in this country has ever held, or even suggested, that prosecutions for libel on government have any place in the American system of jurisprudence. The present proposition would sidestep this obstacle by transmuting criticism of government, however impersonal it may seem on its face, into personal criticism, and hence potential libel, of the officials of whom the government is composed. There is no legal alchemy by which a State may thus create the cause of action that would otherwise be denied for a publication which, as respondent himself said of the advertisement, 'reflects not only on me but on the other Commissioners and the community.' Raising as it does the possibility that a good faith critic of government will be penalized for his criticism, the proposition relied on by the Alabama courts strikes at the very center of the constitutionally protected area of free expression. We hold that such a proposition may not constitutionally be utilized to establish that an otherwise impersonal attack on governmental operations was a libel of an official responsible for those operations. Since it was relied on exclusively here, and there was no other evidence to connect the statements with respondent, the evidence was constitutionally insufficient to support a finding that the statements referred to respondent."

CONCURRING OPINION BY JUSTICE HUGO BLACK

"I concur in reversing this half-million-dollar judgment against the New York Times Company and the four individual defendants. In reversing, the Court holds that the Constitution delimits a State's power to award damages for libel in actions brought by public officials against critics of their official conduct.

"I base my vote to reverse on the belief that the First and Fourteenth Amendments not merely 'delimit' a State's power to award damages to 'public officials against critics of their official conduct,' but completely prohibit a State from exercising such a power. The Court goes on to hold that a State can subject such critics to damages if 'actual malice' can be proved against them. 'Malice,' even as defined by the Court, is an elusive, abstract concept, hard to prove and hard to disprove. The requirement that malice be proved provides, at best, an evanescent protection for the right critically to discuss public affairs, and certainly does not measure up to the sturdy safeguard embodied in the First Amendment. Unlike the Court, therefore, I vote to reverse exclusively on the ground that the Times and the individual defendants had an absolute, unconditional constitutional right to publish in the *Times* advertisement their criticisms of the Montgomery agencies and officials. . . .

"The half-million-dollar verdict does give dramatic proof, however, that state libel laws threaten the very existence of an American press virile enough to publish unpopular views on public affairs and bold enough to criticize the conduct of public officials. . . .

"In my opinion, the Federal Constitution has dealt with this deadly danger to the press in the only way possible without leaving the free press open to destruction—by granting the press an absolute immunity for criticism of the way public officials do their public duty. Stopgap measures like those the Court adopts are, in my judgment, not enough. This record certainly does not indicate that any different verdict would have been rendered here whatever the Court had charged the jury about 'malice,' 'truth,' 'good motives,' 'justifiable ends,' or any other legal formulas which, in theory, would protect the press. Nor does the record indicate that any of these legalistic words would have caused the courts below to set aside or to reduce the half-million-dollar verdict in any amount."

CONCURRING OPINION
BY JUSTICE ARTHUR GOLDBERG

"In my view, the First and Fourteenth Amendments to the Constitution afford to the citizen and to the press an absolute, unconditional privilege to criticize official conduct despite the harm which may flow from excesses and abuses. The prized American right 'to speak one's mind' about public officials and affairs needs 'breathing space to survive.' The right should not depend upon a probing by the jury of the motivation of the citizen or press. The theory of our Constitution is that every citizen may speak his mind and every newspaper express its view on matters of public concern, and may not be barred from speaking or publishing because those in control of government think that what is said or written is unwise, unfair, false, or malicious. In a democratic society, one who assumes to act for the citizens in an executive, legislative, or judicial capacity must expect that his official acts will be commented upon and criticized. Such criticism cannot, in my opinion, be muzzled or deterred by the courts at the instance of public officials under the label of libel.

"It has been recognized that 'prosecutions for libel on government have [no] place in the American system of jurisprudence.' I fully agree. Government, however, is not an abstraction; it is made up of individuals—of governors responsible to the governed. In a democratic society, where men are free by ballots to remove those in power, any statement critical of governmental action is necessarily 'of and concerning' the governors, and any statement critical of the governors' official conduct is necessarily 'of and concerning' the government. If the rule that libel on government has no place in our Constitution is to have real meaning, then libel on the official conduct of the governors likewise can have no place in our Constitution."

★ ★ ★

MIRANDA v. ARIZONA

- 1966 -

★   **RIGHT TO COUNSEL**   ★

The high court established a strict rule of conduct for law enforcement officers by requiring them to tell criminal suspects that they are not required to answer questions without a lawyer present and that a lawyer will be provided if they cannot afford one.

ou have the right to remain silent" is a phrase familiar to anyone who watches police or courtroom dramas. Recited by police before they interrogate suspects, the admonition is the direct result of one of the best-known and most controversial decisions in the Supreme Court's history, *Miranda v. Arizona*.

Ernesto Miranda, then twenty-three, was arrested in 1963 in Phoenix, Arizona, after the kidnapping and rape of a young woman. He denied any involvement at first, but after two hours of police questioning, he confessed. Police did not tell Miranda that he had the right to have an attorney present, so at trial his lawyer said the confession should not be admitted into evidence. It was, and he was convicted.

Miranda's appeal reached the Supreme Court at a time when the justices were increasingly sympathetic to the rights of criminal defendants. In siding with Miranda, the court majority invoked the Fifth Amendment to the Constitution, which said that no criminal suspect can be forced by government to be "a witness against himself."

Chief Justice Earl Warren felt this individual right was so fundamental that police should be told explicitly what to say to suspects before interrogation can begin. To enforce the new rule, the court added that if the "Miranda warning" was not properly given, any resulting confession would not be admitted as evidence.

Joining Warren in the majority were Justices Hugo Black, William O. Douglas, William Brennan Jr., and Abe Fortas. Justices Tom Clark, John Harlan, Byron White, and Potter Stewart dissented. Justice White's dissent predicted that the new rule would undermine the ability of police to interrogate suspects and will, in an unknown number of cases, "return a killer, a rapist or other criminal to the streets."

Law enforcement officials protested at first, but over time the ruling has become accepted, and some commentators say it spurred increased training and professionalism among police nationwide.

As for Miranda, he was tried and convicted again, without using the confession against him. In 1976, Miranda was murdered in a fight at a Phoenix bar. Some news reports stated that he had several "Miranda cards," containing the police warning his case had inspired, in his pocket when he died.

DECISION OF THE COURT
BY CHIEF JUSTICE EARL WARREN

"Our holding will be spelled out with some specificity in the pages which follow, but, briefly stated, it is this: the prosecution may not use statements, whether exculpatory or inculpatory, stemming from custodial interrogation of the defendant unless it demonstrates the use of procedural safeguards effective to secure the privilege against self-incrimination. By custodial interrogation, we mean questioning initiated by law enforcement officers after a person has been taken into custody or otherwise deprived of his freedom of action in any significant way. As for the procedural safeguards to be employed, unless other fully effective means are devised to inform accused persons of their right of silence and to assure a continuous opportunity to exercise it, the following measures are required. Prior to any questioning, the person must be warned that he has a right to remain silent, that any statement he does make may be used as evidence against him, and that he has a right to the presence of an attorney, either retained or appointed. The defendant may waive effectuation of these rights, provided the waiver is made voluntarily, knowingly and intelligently. If, however, he indicates in any manner and at any stage of the process that he wishes to consult with an attorney before speaking, there can be no questioning. Likewise, if the individual is alone and indicates in any manner that he does not wish to be interrogated, the police may not question him. The mere fact that he may have answered some questions or volunteered some statements on his own does not deprive him of the right to refrain from answering any further inquiries until he has consulted with an attorney and thereafter consents to be questioned. . . .

". . . The current practice of incommunicado interrogation is at odds with one of our Nation's most cherished principles—that the individual may not be compelled to incriminate himself. Unless adequate protective devices are employed to dispel the compulsion inherent in custodial surroundings, no statement obtained from the defendant can truly be the product of his free choice. . . .

". . . [T]he privilege against self-incrimination—the essential mainstay of our adversary system—is founded on a complex of values. All these policies point to one overriding thought: the constitutional foundation underlying the privilege is the respect a government—state or federal—must accord to the dignity and integrity of its citizens. To maintain a 'fair state-individual balance,' to require the government 'to shoulder the entire load,' to respect the inviolability of the human personality, our accusatory system of criminal justice demands that the government seeking to punish an individual produce the evidence against him by its own independent labors, rather than by the cruel, simple expedient of compelling it from his own mouth. . . .

"The Fifth Amendment privilege is so fundamental to our system of constitutional rule, and the expedient of giving an adequate warning as to the availability of the privilege so simple, we will not pause to inquire in individual cases whether the defendant was aware of his rights without a warning being given. Assessments of the knowledge the defendant possessed, based on information as to his age, education, intelligence, or prior contact with authorities, can never be more than speculation; a warning is a clear-cut fact. More important, whatever the background of the person interrogated, a warning at the time of the interrogation is indispensable to overcome its pressures and to insure that the individual knows he is free to exercise the privilege at that point in time.

"The warning of the right to remain silent must be accompanied by the explanation that anything said can and will be used against the individual in court. This warning is needed in order to make him aware not only of the privilege, but also of the consequences of forgoing it. It is only through an awareness of these consequences that there can be any assurance of real understanding and intelligent exercise of the privilege. Moreover, this warning may serve to make the individual more acutely aware that he is faced with a phase of the adversary system—that he is not in the presence of persons acting solely in his interest.

"The circumstances surrounding in-custody interrogation can operate very quickly to overbear the will of one merely made aware of his privilege by his interrogators. Therefore, the right to have counsel present at the interrogation is indispensable to the protection of the Fifth Amendment privilege under the system we delineate today. Our aim is to assure that the individual's right to choose between silence and speech remains unfettered throughout the interrogation process. . . .

"Accordingly, we hold that an individual held for interrogation must be clearly informed that he has the right to consult with a lawyer and to have the lawyer with him during interrogation under the system for protecting the privilege we delineate today. As with the warnings of the right to remain silent and that anything stated can be used in evidence against him, this warning is an absolute prerequisite to interrogation. No amount of circumstantial evidence that the person may have been aware of this right will suffice to stand in its stead. Only through such a warning is there ascertainable assurance that the accused was aware of this right. . . .

"The warnings required and the waiver necessary in accordance with our opinion today are, in the absence of a fully effective equivalent, prerequisites to the admissibility of any statement made by a defendant."

DISSENTING OPINION BY JUSTICE TOM CLARK

"Now the Court fashions a constitutional rule that the police may engage in no custodial interrogation without additionally advising the accused that he has a right under the Fifth Amendment to the presence of counsel during interrogation and that, if he is without funds, counsel will be furnished him. When, at any point during an interrogation, the accused seeks affirmatively or impliedly to invoke his rights to silence or counsel, interrogation must be forgone or postponed. The Court further holds that failure to follow the new procedures requires inexorably the exclusion of any statement by the accused, as well as the fruits thereof. Such a strict constitutional specific inserted at the nerve center of crime detection may well kill the patient. Since there is at this time a paucity of information and an almost total lack of empirical knowledge on the practical operation of requirements truly comparable to those announced by the majority, I would be more restrained, lest we go too far too fast. . . .

"Rather than employing the arbitrary Fifth Amendment rule which the Court lays down, I would follow the more pliable dictates of the Due Process Clauses of the Fifth and Fourteenth Amendments which we are accustomed to administering, and which we know from our cases are effective instruments in protecting persons in police custody. In this way, we would not be acting in the dark, nor, in one full sweep, changing the traditional rules of custodial interrogation which this Court has for so long recognized as a justifiable and proper tool in balancing individual rights against the rights of society. It will be soon enough to go further when we are able to appraise with somewhat better accuracy the effect of such a holding. . . .

"In conclusion: nothing in the letter or the spirit of the Constitution or in the precedents squares with the heavy-handed and one-sided action that is so precipitously taken by the Court in the name of fulfilling its constitutional responsibilities. The foray which the Court makes today brings to mind the wise and farsighted words of Mr. Justice Jackson in *Douglas v. Jeannette*: 'This Court is forever adding new stories to the temples of constitutional law, and the temples have a way of collapsing when one story too many is added.'"

DISSENTING OPINION BY JUSTICE BYRON WHITE

"The obvious underpinning of the Court's decision is a deep-seated distrust of all confessions. As the Court declares that the accused may not be interrogated without counsel present, absent a waiver of the right to counsel, and as the Court all but admonishes the lawyer to advise the accused to remain silent, the result adds up to a judicial judgment that evidence from the accused should not be used against him in any way, whether compelled or not. This is the not so subtle overtone of the opinion—that it is inherently wrong for the police to gather evidence from the accused himself. And this is precisely the nub of this dissent. I see nothing wrong or immoral, and certainly nothing unconstitutional, in the police's asking a suspect whom they have reasonable cause to arrest whether or not he killed his wife, or in confronting him with the evidence on which the arrest was based, at least where he has been plainly advised that he may remain completely silent. . . . Particularly when corroborated, as where the police have confirmed the accused's disclosure of the hiding place of implements or fruits of the crime, such confessions have the highest reliability, and significantly contribute to the certitude with which we may believe the accused is guilty. . . .

"The rule announced today will measurably weaken the ability of the criminal law to perform these tasks. It is a deliberate calculus to prevent interrogations, to reduce the incidence of confessions and pleas of guilty, and to increase the number of trials. Criminal trials, no matter how efficient the police are, are not sure bets for the prosecution, nor should they be if the evidence is not forthcoming. . . . But it is something else again to remove from the ordinary criminal case all those confessions which heretofore have been held to be free and voluntary acts of the accused, and to thus establish a new constitutional barrier to the ascertainment of truth by the judicial process.

"There is, in my view, every reason to believe that a good many criminal defendants who otherwise would have been convicted on what this Court has previously thought to be the most satisfactory kind of evidence will now, under this new version of the

Fifth Amendment, either not be tried at all or will be acquitted if the State's evidence, minus the confession, is put to the test of litigation.

"I have no desire whatsoever to share the responsibility for any such impact on the present criminal process.

"In some unknown number of cases, the Court's rule will return a killer, a rapist or other criminal to the streets and to the environment which produced him, to repeat his crime whenever it pleases him. As a consequence, there will not be a gain, but a loss, in human dignity. The real concern is not the unfortunate consequences of this new decision on the criminal law as an abstract, disembodied series of authoritative proscriptions, but the impact on those who rely on the public authority for protection, and who, without it, can only engage in violent self-help with guns, knives and the help of their neighbors similarly inclined. There is, of course, a saving factor: the next victims are uncertain, unnamed and unrepresented in this case."

★　★　★

TINKER v. DES MOINES INDEPENDENT COMMUNITY SCHOOL DISTRICT

- 1969 -

 ★ **STUDENT FREE SPEECH** ★

By declaring that public schools "may not be enclaves of totalitarianism," the Supreme Court established a rule that has set the tone ever since for public schools as places where a significant degree of free expression can flourish.

The 1960s were turbulent times in public schools as well as throughout society. The Vietnam War and the civil rights movement compelled students nationwide to express their views in ways that had rarely been seen before.

Against that backdrop, it would have been hard to predict that a relatively quiet protest against the

Vietnam War by a small group of students in Des Moines, Iowa, in December 1965 would result in a major Supreme Court pronouncement on students' constitutional rights.

The Des Moines students decided to wear black armbands to school to draw attention to the growing number of deaths—civilian and military—in the war.

"We didn't think it was going to be that big of a deal," Mary Beth Tinker wrote later. But word spread, and school officials decided that wearing an armband would be cause for suspension. Tinker, then an eighth grader, was suspended along with her brother John, who was in high school, and another student.

With the aid of the Iowa Civil Liberties Union, parents supporting the suspended students filed suit in federal court, alleging a First Amendment violation. The case made its way to a liberal Supreme Court that was expanding freedoms guaranteed by the Bill of Rights, including the First Amendment.

But arguments that the court should defer to school officials on questions of discipline made the case difficult to decide. Justice Hugo Black, known as a strong defender of First Amendment rights, surprisingly made an exception in the *Tinker* case by voting in favor of the school district.

The court ruled 7–2 in favor of student rights, with Justice Abe Fortas writing the majority opinion. Fortas was joined by Chief Justice Earl Warren and Justices William O. Douglas, William Brennan Jr., Thurgood Marshall, Potter Stewart, and Byron White. White and Stewart wrote brief concurring opinions. Justices Hugo Black and John Harlan wrote separate dissents voicing concern about a breakdown of student discipline.

The *Tinker* ruling has been called the "*Roe v. Wade* for public school students," and it launched an era of considerable freedom for students and teachers in the public school setting. But the court gradually reined in that freedom in a series of decisions that culminated in the 1988 ruling in *Hazelwood School District v. Kuhlmeier*. In that decision, the court said that officials of a Missouri school district did not violate the First Amendment when they censored articles in a high school student newspaper dealing with divorce and teen pregnancy.

The next test of the strength of the *Tinker* ruling may come in the context of student expression online, and whether school officials can ban offensive social media postings that are written outside of school property but pertain to school matters.

DECISION OF THE COURT BY JUSTICE ABE FORTAS

"First Amendment rights, applied in light of the special characteristics of the school environment, are available to teachers and students. It can hardly be argued that either students or teachers shed their constitutional rights to freedom of speech or expression at the schoolhouse gate. This has been the unmistakable holding of this Court for almost 50 years. . . .

"In *West Virginia v. Barnette*, this Court held that, under the First Amendment, the student in public school may not be compelled to salute the flag. Speaking through Mr. Justice Jackson, the Court said: 'The Fourteenth Amendment, as now applied to the States, protects the citizen against the State itself and all of its creatures—Boards of Education not excepted. . . . That they are educating the young for citizenship is reason for scrupulous protection of Constitutional freedoms of the individual, if we are not to strangle the free mind at its source and teach youth to discount important principles of our government as mere platitudes.'

"On the other hand, the Court has repeatedly emphasized the need for affirming the comprehensive authority of the States and of school officials, consistent with fundamental constitutional safeguards, to prescribe and control conduct in the schools. Our problem lies in the area where students in the exercise of First Amendment rights collide with the rules of the school authorities. . . .

"The school officials banned and sought to punish petitioners for a silent, passive expression of opinion, unaccompanied by any disorder or disturbance on the part of petitioners. There is here no evidence whatever of petitioners' interference, actual or nascent, with the schools' work or of collision with the rights of other students to be secure and to be let alone. Accordingly, this case does not concern speech or action that intrudes upon the work of the schools or the rights of other students. . . .

". . .[I]n our system, undifferentiated fear or apprehension of disturbance is not enough to overcome the right to freedom of expression. Any departure from absolute regimentation may cause trouble. Any variation from the majority's opinion may inspire fear. Any word spoken, in class, in the lunchroom, or on the campus, that deviates from the views of another person may start an argument or cause a disturbance. But our Constitution says we must take this risk. . . .

". . . Certainly where there is no finding and no showing that engaging in the forbidden conduct would 'materially and substantially interfere with the requirements of appropriate discipline in the operation of the school,' the prohibition cannot be sustained. . . .

"In our system, state-operated schools may not be enclaves of totalitarianism. School officials do not possess absolute authority over their students. Students in school, as well as out of school, are 'persons' under our Constitution. They are possessed of fundamental rights which the State must respect, just as they themselves must respect their obligations to the State. In our system, students may not be regarded as closed-circuit recipients of only that which the State chooses to communicate. They may not be confined to the expression of those sentiments that are officially approved. In the absence of a specific showing of constitutionally valid reasons to regulate their speech, students are entitled to freedom of expression of their views. . . .

". . . The principal use to which the schools are dedicated is to accommodate students during prescribed hours for the purpose of certain types of activities. Among those activities is personal intercommunication among the students. This is not only an inevitable part of the process of attending school; it is also an important part of the educational process. A student's rights, therefore, do not embrace merely the classroom hours. When he is in the cafeteria, or on the playing field, or on the campus during the authorized hours, he may express his opinions, even on controversial subjects like the conflict in Vietnam, if he does so without 'materially and substantially interfer[ing] with the requirements of appropriate discipline in the operation of the school' and without colliding with the rights of others. . . .

"Under our Constitution, free speech is not a right that is given only to be so circumscribed that it exists in principle, but not in fact. Freedom of expression would not truly exist if the right could be exercised only in an area that a benevolent government has provided as a safe haven for crackpots. The Constitution says that Congress (and the States) may not abridge the right to free speech. This provision means what it says. We properly read it to permit reasonable regulation of speech-connected activities in carefully restricted circumstances. But we do not confine the permissible exercise of First Amendment rights to a telephone booth or the four corners of a pamphlet, or to supervised and ordained discussion in a school classroom."

CONCURRING OPINION BY JUSTICE POTTER STEWART

"Although I agree with much of what is said in the Court's opinion, and with its judgment in this case,

I cannot share the Court's uncritical assumption that, school discipline aside, the First Amendment rights of children are coextensive with those of adults. Indeed, I had thought the Court decided otherwise just last Term in *Ginsberg v. New York*. I continue to hold the view I expressed in that case:

"[A] State may permissibly determine that, at least in some precisely delineated areas, a child—like someone in a captive audience—is not possessed of that full capacity for individual choice which is the presupposition of First Amendment guarantees."

CONCURRING OPINION BY JUSTICE BYRON WHITE

"While I join the Court's opinion, I deem it appropriate to note, first, that the Court continues to recognize a distinction between communicating by words and communicating by acts or conduct which sufficiently impinges on some valid state interest; and, second, that I do not subscribe to everything the Court of Appeals said about free speech in its opinion in *Burnside v. Byars*, a case relied upon by the Court in the matter now before us."

DISSENTING OPINION BY JUSTICE HUGO BLACK

"The Court's holding in this case ushers in what I deem to be an entirely new era in which the power to control pupils by the elected 'officials of state supported public schools . . .' in the United States is in ultimate effect transferred to the Supreme

Court. . . . Here, the constitutional right to 'political expression' asserted was a right to wear black armbands during school hours and at classes in order to demonstrate to the other students that the petitioners were mourning because of the death of United States soldiers in Vietnam and to protest that war which they were against. Ordered to refrain from wearing the armbands in school by the elected school officials and the teachers vested with state authority to do so, apparently only seven out of the school system's 18,000 pupils deliberately refused to obey the order. . . .

"Assuming that the Court is correct in holding that the conduct of wearing armbands for the purpose of conveying political ideas is protected by the First Amendment, the crucial remaining questions are whether students and teachers may use the schools at their whim as a platform for the exercise of free speech—'symbolic' or 'pure'—and whether the courts will allocate to themselves the function of deciding how the pupils' school day will be spent. While I have always believed that, under the First and Fourteenth Amendments, neither the State nor the Federal Government has any authority to regulate or censor the content of speech, I have never believed that any person has a right to give speeches or engage in demonstrations where he pleases and when he pleases. . . .

"While the record does not show that any of these armband students shouted, used profane language, or were violent in any manner, detailed testimony by some of them shows their armbands caused comments, warnings by other students, the poking of fun at them, and a warning by an older football player that other nonprotesting students had better let them alone. . . . While the absence of obscene remarks or boisterous and loud disorder perhaps justifies the Court's statement that the few armband students did not actually 'disrupt' the classwork, I think the record overwhelmingly shows that the armbands did exactly what the elected school officials and principals foresaw they would, that is, took the students' minds off their classwork and diverted them to thoughts about the highly emotional subject of the Vietnam war. And I repeat that, if the time has come when pupils of state-supported schools, kindergartens, grammar schools, or high schools, can defy and flout orders of school officials to keep their minds on their own schoolwork, it is the beginning of a new revolutionary era of permissiveness in this country fostered by the judiciary. The next logical step, it appears to me, would be to hold unconstitutional laws that bar pupils under 21 or 18 from voting, or from being elected members of the boards of education."

DISSENTING OPINION
BY JUSTICE JOHN MARSHALL HARLAN

"I certainly agree that state public school authorities, in the discharge of their responsibilities, are not wholly exempt from the requirements of the Fourteenth Amendment respecting the freedoms of expression and association. At the same time, I am reluctant to believe that there is any disagreement between the majority and myself on the proposition that school officials should be accorded the widest authority in maintaining discipline and good order in their institutions. To translate that proposition into a workable constitutional rule, I would, in cases like this, cast upon those complaining the burden of showing that a particular school measure was motivated by other than legitimate school concerns—for example, a desire to prohibit the expression of an unpopular point of view, while permitting expression of the dominant opinion.

"Finding nothing in this record which impugns the good faith of respondents in promulgating the armband regulation, I would affirm the judgment below."

★　★　★

FURMAN v. GEORGIA

- 1972 -

★   **CAPITAL PUNISHMENT**   ★

For the first time, the court ruled that the death penalty as then carried out violated the Eighth Amendment of the Constitution, which prohibits "cruel and unusual punishments."

The U.S. Constitution was drafted at a time when capital punishment was routinely accepted as punishment for offenses ranging from murder to forgery. The Bill of Rights indirectly acknowledged its existence when it said that government could not deprive persons of "life, liberty or property without due process." Some scholars concluded from this history that the death penalty was clearly constitutional.

But over time, abolitionists began pointing to a different part of the Bill of Rights to argue that capital punishment could be found unconstitutional under modern-day norms and views of morality and human dignity. The Eighth Amendment prohibits punishments that are "cruel and unusual"—adjectives that seem to require consideration of subjective opinions, changing attitudes about morality, and modern-day practices. Hanging may have once been a common or seemingly humane way to execute criminals but now most Americans would probably agree that it is both "cruel and unusual."

In 1968, the court recognized the subjective nature of the words of the Eighth Amendment when it said in *Trop v. Dulles*, "The amendment must draw its meaning from the evolving standards of decency that mark the progress of a maturing society."

The civil rights movement of the 1960s helped trigger new efforts to curtail or abolish the death penalty, in part because black defendants were the most likely to be sentenced to death. In 1971 three challenges made their way to the U.S. Supreme Court—two from Georgia and one from Texas. The cases were consolidated under the name *Furman v. Georgia*.

It was a difficult decision for the court to make, resulting in separate written opinions by all nine justices. The five-justice majority asserted several different reasons for finding the punishment "cruel and unusual" as practice at the time, including Justice Potter Stewart's view that the imposition of the death sentence was so random and unpredictable that it was like "being struck by lightning."

The four dissenters objected mainly on the grounds that whether the death penalty should be ended was a matter for state legislators to decide—not the sudden whim of five unelected Supreme Court justices.

The decision generated instant controversy. State legislatures quickly began revising their laws in ways that would reduce the arbitrariness of the death penalty that bothered the court. Inevitably, challenges to the new laws came back to the high court.

In the 1976 decision *Gregg v. Georgia*, the court endorsed some of the new laws, and executions resumed. But the debate over the death penalty was far from over. In the last forty years, the court has prohibited the death penalty for crimes that do not involve murder, and for certain categories of defendants such as juveniles and the intellectually disabled.

Individual justices, meanwhile, continued to struggle with the issue. Justices Harry Blackmun and John Paul Stevens, both appointees of Republican presidents, turned against capital punishment. In a 2015 dissent, Justice Stephen Breyer cited the "serious unreliability" of the penalty and the "unconscionable delay" in executions as reasons for the court to take another look at its constitutionality. Justice Ruth Bader Ginsburg was the only other justice to join his dissent.

UNSIGNED DECISION OF THE COURT

"The Court holds that the imposition and carrying out of the death penalty in these cases constitute cruel and unusual punishment in violation of the

Eighth and Fourteenth Amendments. The judgment in each case is therefore reversed insofar as it leaves undisturbed the death sentence imposed, and the cases are remanded for further proceedings."

CONCURRING OPINION
BY JUSTICE WILLIAM O. DOUGLAS

"We deal with a system of law and of justice that leaves to the uncontrolled discretion of judges or juries the determination whether defendants committing these crimes should die or be imprisoned. Under these laws no standards govern the selection of the penalty. People live or die, dependent on the whim of one man or of 12. . . .

"A law that stated that anyone making more than $50,000 would be exempt from the death penalty would plainly fall, as would a law that in terms said that blacks, those who never went beyond the fifth grade in school, those who made less than $3,000 a year, or those who were unpopular or unstable should be the only people executed. A law which in the overall view reaches that result in practice has no more sanctity than a law which in terms provides the same.

"Thus, these discretionary statutes are unconstitutional in their operation. They are pregnant with discrimination, and discrimination is an ingredient not compatible with the idea of equal protection of the laws that is implicit in the ban on 'cruel and unusual' punishments."

CONCURRING OPINION
BY JUSTICE WILLIAM BRENNAN JR.

"The Cruel and Unusual Punishments Clause prohibits the infliction of uncivilized and inhuman punishments. The State, even as it punishes, must treat its members with respect for their intrinsic worth as human beings. A punishment is 'cruel and unusual,' therefore, if it does not comport with human dignity. . . .

"In determining whether a punishment comports with human dignity, we are aided also by a second principle inherent in the Clause—that the State must not arbitrarily inflict a severe punishment. This principle derives from the notion that the State does not respect human dignity when, without reason, it inflicts upon some people a severe punishment that it does not inflict upon others. Indeed, the very words 'cruel and unusual punishments' imply condemnation of the arbitrary infliction of severe punishments."

CONCURRING OPINION
BY JUSTICE POTTER STEWART

"These death sentences are cruel and unusual in the same way that being struck by lightning is cruel and unusual. For, of all the people convicted of rapes and murders in 1967 and 1968, many just as reprehensible as these, the petitioners are among a capriciously selected random handful upon whom the sentence of death has in fact been imposed. My concurring Brothers have demonstrated that, if any basis can be discerned for the selection of these few to be sentenced to die, it is the constitutionally impermissible basis of race. But racial discrimination has not been proved, and I put it to one side. I simply conclude that the Eighth and Fourteenth Amendments cannot tolerate the infliction of a sentence of death under legal systems that permit this unique penalty to be so wantonly and so freakishly imposed."

CONCURRING OPINION
BY JUSTICE BYRON WHITE

"I can do no more than state a conclusion based on 10 years of almost daily exposure to the facts and circumstances of hundreds and hundreds of federal and state criminal cases involving crimes for which death is the authorized penalty. That conclusion, as I have said, is that the death penalty is exacted with great infrequency even for the most atrocious crimes and that there is no meaningful basis for distinguishing the few cases in which it is imposed from the many cases in which it is not. The short of it is that the policy of vesting sentencing authority primarily in juries—a decision largely motivated by the desire to mitigate the harshness of the law and to bring community judgment to bear on the sentence as well as guilt or innocence—has so effectively achieved its aims that capital punishment within the confines of the statutes now before us has, for all practical purposes, run its course."

CONCURRING OPINION
BY JUSTICE THURGOOD MARSHALL

"The criminal acts with which we are confronted are ugly, vicious, reprehensible acts. Their sheer brutality cannot and should not be minimized. But, we are not called upon to condone the penalized conduct; we are asked only to examine the penalty imposed on each of the petitioners and to determine whether or not it violates the Eighth Amendment. The question then is not whether we condone rape or murder, for surely we do not; it is whether capital punishment is 'a punishment no longer consistent with our own self-respect' and, therefore, violative of the Eighth Amendment. . . .

"It has often been noted that American citizens know almost nothing about capital punishment. Some of the conclusions arrived at in the preceding section and the supporting evidence would be critical to an informed judgment on the morality of the death penalty: e.g., that the death penalty is no more effective a deterrent than life imprisonment, that convicted murderers are rarely executed, but are usually sentenced to a term in prison; that convicted murderers usually are model prisoners, and that they almost always become law-abiding citizens upon their release from prison; that the costs of executing a capital offender exceed the costs of imprisoning him for life; that while in prison, a convict under sentence of death performs none of the useful functions that life prisoners perform; that no attempt is made in the sentencing process to ferret out likely recidivists for execution; and that the death penalty may actually stimulate criminal activity."

DISSENTING OPINION
BY CHIEF JUSTICE WARREN BURGER

"There are no obvious indications that capital punishment offends the conscience of society to such a degree that our traditional deference to the legislative judgment must be abandoned. . . .

". . . The Eighth Amendment forbids the imposition of punishments that are so cruel and inhumane as to violate society's standards of civilized conduct. The Amendment does not prohibit all punishments the States are unable to prove necessary to deter or control crime. The Amendment is not concerned with the process by which a State determines that a particular punishment is to be imposed in a particular case. And the Amendment most assuredly does not speak to the power of legislatures to confer sentencing discretion on juries, rather than to fix all sentences by statute."

DISSENTING OPINION
BY JUSTICE LEWIS POWELL JR.

"In terms of the constitutional role of this Court, the impact of the majority's ruling is all the greater because the decision encroaches upon an area squarely within the historic prerogative of the legislative branch—both state and federal—to protect the citizenry through the designation of penalties for prohibitable conduct. It is the very sort of judgment that the legislative branch is competent to make, and for which the judiciary is ill-equipped. Throughout our history, Justices of this Court have emphasized the gravity of decisions invalidating legislative judgments, admonishing the nine men who sit on this bench of the duty of self-restraint, especially when called upon to apply the expansive due process and cruel and unusual punishment rubrics. I can recall no case in which, in the name of deciding constitutional questions, this Court has subordinated national and local democratic processes to such an extent."

DISSENTING OPINION
BY JUSTICE HARRY BLACKMUN

"Cases such as these provide for me an excruciating agony of the spirit. I yield to no one in the depth of my distaste, antipathy, and, indeed, abhorrence, for the death penalty, with all its aspects of physical distress and fear and of moral judgment exercised by finite minds. That distaste is buttressed by a belief that capital punishment serves no useful purpose that can be demonstrated. . . . Were I a legislator, I would vote against the death penalty. . . .

"I do not sit on these cases, however, as a legislator, responsive, at least in part, to the will of constituents. Our task here, as must so frequently be emphasized and re-emphasized, is to pass upon the constitutionality of legislation that has been enacted and that is challenged. This is the sole task for judges."

DISSENTING OPINION
BY JUSTICE WILLIAM REHNQUIST

"The Court's judgments today strike down a penalty that our Nation's legislators have thought necessary since our country was founded. My Brothers Douglas, Brennan, and Marshall would, at one fell swoop, invalidate laws enacted by Congress and 40 of the 50 state legislatures, and would consign to the limbo of unconstitutionality under a single rubric penalties for offenses as varied and unique as murder, piracy, mutiny, highjacking, and desertion in the face of the enemy. My Brothers Stewart and White, asserting reliance on a more limited rationale—the reluctance of judges and juries actually to impose the death penalty in the majority of capital cases—join in the judgments in these cases. Whatever its precise rationale, today's holding necessarily brings into sharp relief the fundamental question of the role of judicial review in a democratic society. How can government by the elected representatives of the people coexist with the power of the federal judiciary, whose members are constitutionally insulated from responsiveness to the popular will, to declare invalid laws duly enacted by the popular branches of government?"

★   ★   ★

ROE v. WADE

- 1973 -

★   **ABORTION RIGHTS**   ★

In a single stroke, the Supreme Court struck down laws in most states that banned abortions except to save the life of the mother. By declaring that women have a constitutional right to choose abortions and control their reproductive lives, the Supreme Court brought about a profound change in American society.

Whether women have a right to an abortion remains one of the most contentious issues in America. It is such a deeply felt religious, moral, and political issue that doctors who perform abortions have been murdered, and state legislators have passed dozens of statutes aimed at restricting the abortion right or banning it altogether. In May 2016, for example, the Oklahoma legislature passed a law making it a felony to perform abortions, which would have effectively ended the practice in the state. Governor Mary Fallin vetoed the legislation as "ambiguous and vague."

Abortion was not always so controversial, Justice Harry Blackmun asserted in his 1973 *Roe v. Wade* decision: "At common law, at the time of the adoption of our Constitution, and throughout the major portion of the 19th century, abortion was viewed with less disfavor than under most American statutes currently in effect." The norms in place at the time of the Constitution's framing are often a key factor in the Supreme Court's decision-making.

But by the mid-twentieth century, many states passed laws banning or severely restricting abortions, triggering a backlash from women's rights advocates. The Supreme Court itself fueled the reaction in 1965 with its *Griswold v. Connecticut* ruling, which struck down a state ban on contraceptives. That decision set forth a right to personal privacy that had not been articulated before and that was crucial to the court's subsequent decision in *Roe*.

Abortion rights advocates recruited Dallas resident Norma McCorvey to challenge the Texas ban on abortions. Her real name was shielded in court papers under the pseudonym Jane Roe. She agreed to initiate a lawsuit challenging the Texas law and filed suit in federal court in 1970, naming Dallas County district attorney Henry Wade as the defendant. The court sided with McCorvey but denied her an injunction to stop enforcement of the law, setting the stage for a Supreme Court showdown on abortion.

Chief Justice Warren Burger assigned the decision to a relatively new justice, Harry Blackmun, who had experience with medical issues as the former general counsel of the Mayo Clinic.

Blackmun rooted the decision favoring abortion rights in the Fourteenth Amendment's guarantee that government shall not "deprive any person of life, liberty, or property, without due process of law." That concept of personal liberty, he said, encompasses the right of women to choose abortions at the early stages of pregnancy. The state's interest in the life of the child increases, however, as the fetus reaches the point of viability—the ability to live outside the womb.

The court majority avoided the contentious issue of when human life begins. "When those trained in the respective disciplines of medicine, philosophy, and theology are unable to arrive at any consensus, the judiciary, at this point in the development of man's knowledge, is not in a position to speculate as to the answer," Blackmun wrote.

Justice Potter Stewart wrote a concurrence to the majority opinion, and Justice William Rehnquist was the only dissenter. Rehnquist argued that the concept of privacy is not involved in the abortion decision, and that the court's division of pregnancy into three trimesters where different rules apply amounts to "judicial legislation."

The *Roe* ruling had the immediate and dramatic effect of striking down laws across the country that restricted or banned abortions. Women's rights advocates and others applauded the decision for giving women control over their reproductive lives as well as new opportunities to shape their personal and professional lives. Religious leaders and conservatives attacked the ruling for cheapening the value of human life.

The legal battle to overturn *Roe* or restrict abortions in other ways has continued ever since the ruling. With the advent of a more conservative lineup of justices in recent years, some of those restrictions have been upheld—though the basic right to abortion has not been overruled.

In June 2016, the Supreme Court issued an important ruling on abortion rights, titled *Whole Woman's Health v. Hellerstedt*. By a 5–3 vote, the court struck down regulations imposed on abortion clinics in Texas that would have closed down many facilities throughout the state. Justice Anthony Kennedy, who had long supported restrictions on abortions, switched sides in the case, joining the majority in finding that the restrictions posed an "undue burden" on women's access to abortions. Some commentators said the decision places the abortion right first declared in *Roe* on the firmest footing ever.

DECISION OF THE COURT
BY JUSTICE HARRY BLACKMUN

"We forthwith acknowledge our awareness of the sensitive and emotional nature of the abortion controversy, of the vigorous opposing views, even among physicians, and of the deep and seemingly absolute convictions that the subject inspires. One's philosophy, one's experiences, one's exposure to the raw edges of human existence, one's religious training, one's attitudes toward life and family and their values, and the moral standards one establishes and seeks to observe, are all likely to influence and to color one's thinking and conclusions about abortion.

"In addition, population growth, pollution, poverty, and racial overtones tend to complicate and not to simplify the problem.

"Our task, of course, is to resolve the issue by constitutional measurement, free of emotion and of predilection. We seek earnestly to do this, and, because we do, we have inquired into, and in this opinion place some emphasis upon, medical and medical-legal history and what that history reveals about man's attitudes toward the abortion procedure over the centuries. . . .

"The Constitution does not explicitly mention any right of privacy. In a line of decisions, however, going back perhaps as far as *Union Pacific R. Co. v. Botsford* (1891), the Court has recognized that a right of personal privacy, or a guarantee of certain areas or zones of privacy, does exist under the Constitution. . . .

"This right of privacy, whether it be founded in the Fourteenth Amendment's concept of personal liberty and restrictions upon state action, as we feel it is, or, as the District Court determined, in the Ninth Amendment's reservation of rights to the people, is broad enough to encompass a woman's decision whether or not to terminate her pregnancy. . . .

". . . The Court's decisions recognizing a right of privacy also acknowledge that some state regulation in areas protected by that right is appropriate. . . . A State may properly assert important interests in safeguarding health, in maintaining medical standards, and in protecting potential life. At some point in pregnancy, these respective interests become sufficiently compelling to sustain regulation of the factors that govern the abortion decision. The privacy right involved, therefore, cannot be said to be absolute. . . .

"With respect to the State's important and legitimate interest in the health of the mother, the 'compelling' point, in the light of present medical knowledge, is at approximately the end of the first trimester. This is so because of the now-established medical fact . . . that, until the end of the first trimester, mortality in abortion may be less than mortality in normal childbirth. It follows that, from and after this point, a State may regulate the abortion procedure to the extent that the regulation reasonably relates to the preservation and protection of maternal health. Examples of permissible state regulation in this area are requirements as to the qualifications of the person who is to perform the abortion; as to the licensure of that person; as to the facility in which the procedure is to be performed, that is, whether it must be a hospital or may be a clinic or some other place of less-than-hospital status; as to the licensing of the facility; and the like."

CONCURRING OPINION
BY JUSTICE POTTER STEWART

"The Court today is correct in holding that the right asserted by Jane Roe is embraced within the personal liberty protected by the Due Process Clause of the Fourteenth Amendment.

"It is evident that the Texas abortion statute infringes that right directly. Indeed, it is difficult to imagine a more complete abridgment of a constitutional freedom than that worked by the inflexible criminal statute now in force in Texas. The question then becomes whether the state interests advanced to justify this abridgment can survive the 'particularly careful scrutiny' that the Fourteenth Amendment here requires.

"The asserted state interests are protection of the health and safety of the pregnant woman, and protection of the potential future human life within her. These are legitimate objectives, amply sufficient to permit a State to regulate abortions as it does other surgical procedures, and perhaps sufficient to permit a State to regulate abortions more stringently, or even to prohibit them in the late stages of pregnancy. But such legislation is not before us, and I think the Court today has thoroughly demonstrated that these state interests cannot constitutionally support the broad abridgment of personal liberty worked by the existing Texas law. Accordingly, I join the Court's opinion holding that that law is invalid under the Due Process Clause of the Fourteenth Amendment."

DISSENTING OPINION
BY JUSTICE WILLIAM REHNQUIST

"The Court's opinion decides that a State may impose virtually no restriction on the performance of abortions during the first trimester of pregnancy. Our previous decisions indicate that a necessary predicate for such an opinion is a plaintiff who was in her first trimester of pregnancy at some time during the pendency of her lawsuit. While a party may vindicate his own constitutional rights, he may not seek vindication for the rights of others. The Court's statement of facts in this case makes clear, however, that the record in no way indicates the presence of such a plaintiff. We know only that plaintiff Roe at the time of filing her complaint was a pregnant woman; for aught that appears in this record, she may have been in her last trimester of pregnancy as of the date the complaint was filed.

"Nothing in the Court's opinion indicates that Texas might not constitutionally apply its proscription of abortion as written to a woman in that stage of pregnancy. Nonetheless, the Court uses her complaint against the Texas statute as a fulcrum for deciding that States may impose virtually no restrictions on medical abortions performed during the first trimester of pregnancy. In deciding such a hypothetical lawsuit, the Court departs from the longstanding admonition that it should never 'formulate a rule of constitutional law broader than is required by the precise facts to which it is to be applied.'

". . . I have difficulty in concluding, as the Court does, that the right of 'privacy' is involved in this case. Texas, by the statute here challenged, bars the performance of a medical abortion by a licensed physician on a plaintiff such as Roe. A transaction resulting in an operation such as this is not 'private' in the ordinary usage of that word. Nor is the 'privacy' that the Court finds here even a distant relative of the freedom from searches and seizures protected by the Fourth Amendment to the Constitution, which the Court has referred to as embodying a right to privacy.

"If the Court means by the term 'privacy' no more than that the claim of a person to be free from unwanted state regulation of consensual transactions may be a form of 'liberty' protected by the Fourteenth Amendment, there is no doubt that similar claims have been upheld in our earlier decisions on the basis of that liberty. I agree with the statement of Mr. Justice Stewart in his concurring opinion that the 'liberty,' against deprivation of which without due process the Fourteenth Amendment protects, embraces more than the rights found in the Bill of Rights. But that liberty is not guaranteed absolutely against deprivation, only against deprivation without due process of law. The test traditionally applied in the area of social and economic legislation is whether or not a law such as that challenged has a rational relation to a valid state objective. . . . But the Court's sweeping invalidation of any restrictions on abortion during the first trimester is impossible to justify under that standard, and the conscious weighing of competing factors that the Court's opinion apparently substitutes for the established test is far more appropriate to a legislative judgment than to a judicial one. . . .

". . . The decision here to break pregnancy into three distinct terms and to outline the permissible restrictions the State may impose in each one, for example, partakes more of judicial legislation than it does of a determination of the intent of the drafters of the Fourteenth Amendment.

"The fact that a majority of the States reflecting, after all, the majority sentiment in those States, have had restrictions on abortions for at least a century is a strong indication, it seems to me, that the asserted right to an abortion is not 'so rooted in the traditions and conscience of our people as to be ranked as fundamental.' Even today, when society's views on abortion are changing, the very existence of the debate is evidence that the 'right' to an abortion is not so universally accepted as the appellant would have us believe.

"To reach its result, the Court necessarily has had to find within the scope of the Fourteenth Amendment a right that was apparently completely unknown to the drafters of the Amendment. As early as 1821, the first state law dealing directly with abortion was enacted by the Connecticut Legislature. By the time of the adoption of the Fourteenth Amendment in 1868, there were at least 36 laws enacted by state or territorial legislatures limiting abortion. While many States have amended or updated their laws, 21 of the laws on the books in 1868 remain in effect today. Indeed, the Texas statute struck down today was, as the majority notes, first enacted in 1857, and 'has remained substantially unchanged to the present time.'

"There apparently was no question concerning the validity of this provision or of any of the other state statutes when the Fourteenth Amendment was adopted. The only conclusion possible from this history is that the drafters did not intend to have the Fourteenth Amendment withdraw from the States the power to legislate with respect to this matter."

★ ★ ★

UNITED STATES
v. NIXON

- 1974 -

★   **PRESIDENTIAL POWER**   ★

Reinforcing the maxim that "No man is above the law," the Supreme Court ruled that President Richard Nixon could not invoke "executive privilege" to disobey a subpoena for audiotapes and documents related to the Watergate scandal.

What started as a bungled burglary of Democratic Party offices in Washington, D.C., in 1972 turned into a constitutional crisis by 1974. In between, the Nixon White House tried to cover up the political motivations for the crime, which took place during the 1972 presidential election campaign that ended up reelecting Nixon for a second term.

Investigative reporting by news media led the administration to appoint a special prosecutor to investigate whether crimes had been committed. When congressional hearings revealed that Nixon had secretly taped conversations in the White House, special prosecutor Archibald Cox sought access to several of the tapes.

Nixon refused and ordered Attorney General Elliot Richardson to fire Cox. In a dramatic series of events that became known as the "Saturday night massacre," Richardson refused to fire Cox, as did his deputy, William Ruckelshaus. Both resigned. Robert Bork, the third-ranking Justice Department official, agreed to fire Cox and return the Watergate investigation to the Justice Department.

But public pressure continued, and Leon Jaworski, a litigator who had served as a prosecutor during the Nuremberg trials, was appointed to replace Cox. Jaworski proceeded to subpoena the tapes again. Nixon offered to provide edited transcripts of the tapes, but that was not enough.

As the standoff moved to the courts, Nixon's lawyers invoked "executive privilege," arguing that presidential communications should not be shared with the other branches of the government. U.S. District Judge John Sirica rejected that argument and upheld the subpoena.

Because of the urgency of the matter, Jaworski then took the case directly to the Supreme Court instead of waiting for an intermediate court to rule. The court agreed and scheduled the arguments for

July 8, even though that would be after the court began its usual summer recess.

In addition to arguing that courts could not second-guess a president's claim of privilege, Nixon's lawyers asserted that because the dispute was within the executive branch, courts had no role to play. But when the justices met privately after the arguments, it was clear that Nixon's arguments had no support. Chief Justice Warren Burger, who had been appointed to the court in 1969 by Nixon, took on the task of writing the opinion that would undercut Nixon's effort to keep his job.

The court unanimously ruled that it had the authority to rule on the executive privilege claim. Burger said presidents deserve the "utmost deference" in keeping their communications private, especially on military, diplomatic, or national security matters. But in the rare occasion when documents are subpoenaed as part of a criminal investigation, that deference falls away.

The Court's unambiguous ruling made Nixon realize that he had no choice but to turn over the subpoenaed materials. But White House officials also knew that the tapes contained "smoking gun" evidence revealing that Nixon discussed with his aides ways to thwart the FBI's investigation of the Watergate episode. That would amount to obstruction of justice, a serious criminal offense.

At the same time, the House Judiciary Committee began voting on articles of impeachment, making Nixon's removal from office seem inevitable. On August 5, transcripts of the damaging conversations were made public, and on August 9, less than three weeks after the Supreme Court ruled, Richard Nixon became the first president in U.S. history to resign from office.

DECISION OF THE COURT
BY CHIEF JUSTICE WARREN BURGER

"Neither the doctrine of separation of powers nor the need for confidentiality of high-level communications, without more, can sustain an absolute, unqualified Presidential privilege of immunity from judicial process under all circumstances. The President's need for complete candor and objectivity from advisers calls for great deference from the courts. However, when the privilege depends solely on the broad, undifferentiated claim of public interest in the confidentiality of such conversations, a confrontation with other values arises. . . .

"The impediment that an absolute, unqualified privilege would place in the way of the primary constitutional duty of the Judicial Branch to do justice in criminal prosecutions would plainly conflict with the function of the courts under Art. III. In designing the structure of our Government and dividing and allocating the sovereign power among three co-equal branches, the Framers of the Constitution sought to provide a comprehensive system, but the separate powers were not intended to operate with absolute independence. . . .

"To read the Art. II powers of the President as providing an absolute privilege as against a subpoena essential to enforcement of criminal statutes on no more than a generalized claim of the public interest in confidentiality of nonmilitary and nondiplomatic discussions would upset the constitutional balance of 'a workable government' and gravely impair the role of the courts under Art. III.

". . . A President and those who assist him must be free to explore alternatives in the process of shaping policies and making decisions, and to do so in a way many would be unwilling to express except privately. These are the considerations justifying a presumptive privilege for Presidential communications. The privilege is fundamental to the operation of Government, and inextricably rooted in the separation of powers under the Constitution. . . .

"But this presumptive privilege must be considered in light of our historic commitment to the rule of law. . . . We have elected to employ an adversary system of criminal justice in which the parties contest all issues before a court of law. The need to develop all relevant facts in the adversary system is both fundamental and comprehensive. . . . To ensure that justice is done, it is imperative to the function of courts that compulsory process be available for the production of evidence needed either by the prosecution or by the defense. . . .

"In this case, we must weigh the importance of the general privilege of confidentiality of Presidential communications in performance of the

President's responsibilities against the inroads of such a privilege on the fair administration of criminal justice. The interest in preserving confidentiality is weighty indeed, and entitled to great respect. However, we cannot conclude that advisers will be moved to temper the candor of their remarks by the infrequent occasions of disclosure because of the possibility that such conversations will be called for in the context of a criminal prosecution.

"On the other hand, the allowance of the privilege to withhold evidence that is demonstrably relevant in a criminal trial would cut deeply into the guarantee of due process of law and gravely impair the basic function of the court. . . . Without access to specific facts, a criminal prosecution may be totally frustrated. The President's broad interest in confidentiality of communications will not be vitiated by disclosure of a limited number of conversations preliminarily shown to have some bearing on the pending criminal cases."

★   ★   ★

REGENTS OF THE UNIVERSITY OF CALIFORNIA v. BAKKE

- 1978 -

★ **AFFIRMATIVE ACTION** ★

The Supreme Court issued a split opinion on the constitutionality of so-called "affirmative action" programs that take race into account as a positive factor in college admissions, hiring, and other benefits. When aimed at remedying past discrimination, such programs are permissible, the court ruled—except when they involve quotas that reserve a certain number of slots for minorities and exclude whites from eligibility.

Affirmative action" programs proliferated during the civil rights movement in the 1960s to compensate for the lingering effects of centuries of racial discrimination, economic disadvantage, and poor school opportunities.

Congress had passed laws prohibiting discrimination in employment, public accommodations, and voting, but Democratic and Republican leaders agreed that more was needed.

President Lyndon Johnson made the case for affirmative action in simple language in a 1966 speech at Howard University. "You do not take a person who, for years, has been hobbled by chains and liberate him, bring him up to the starting line, and then say, 'you are free to compete with all the others,' and still justly believe that you have been completely fair."

But these programs were controversial, especially when they involved quotas that put a specific number of openings beyond the reach of whites. To some, such programs amounted to "reverse discrimination" that violated the Equal Protection Clause of the Fourteenth Amendment.

Allen Bakke symbolized those concerns when he embarked on a career in medicine. In 1973 Bakke, then thirty-three, applied to the University of California at Davis, which twice rejected his application for admission. He learned that the university had set aside sixteen of the one hundred places in its entering class for blacks, Hispanics, Asian-Americans, and Native Americans. Those sixteen spaces were filled through a separate admission process.

Bakke filed suit against the university, claiming he was being discriminated against because he was white. The California Supreme Court ruled that the university admission policy violated the

Fourteenth Amendment and ordered that Bakke be admitted. The university appealed to the U.S. Supreme Court, setting the stage for a landmark ruling on race.

The Supreme Court was deeply split, with four justices ready to strike down the University of California program and four ready to endorse it. Justice Lewis Powell Jr. was ambivalent, but liberal justice William Brennan Jr. suggested a compromise of sorts that Powell agreed to and that formed the basis for the court's opinion.

By creating an "explicit racial classification" for the places reserved for minorities, the university violated the Fourteenth Amendment and Bakke should be admitted, Powell said. But the use of race as one of many factors in a future "properly devised" admissions policy was permissible, in his view.

No other justice joined Powell's opinion in its entirety, but it stood as the opinion of the court. When he read the opinion from the bench, Powell acknowledged that "we speak today with a notable lack of unanimity." Additional opinions by Justices Brennan, Byron White, Thurgood Marshall, Harry Blackmun, and John Paul Stevens detailed the parts of the Powell opinion they did or did not agree with.

The decision did not end the debate over affirmative action by any means. As the high court grew more conservative, it became more and more skeptical of affirmative action. The most dramatic shift came when President George H. W. Bush appointed Clarence Thomas to replace retiring justice Thurgood Marshall, who supported the university program in *Bakke*. Thomas, who, like Marshall, was African-American, had an entirely different view of affirmative action. Drawing on his own experiences in college and law school, Thomas said such programs stigmatize minority students, because their white classmates assume they are not qualified to be admitted without a boost.

In 2003, when another affirmative action case titled *Grutter v. Bollinger* reached the court, some believed it would spell the end of such programs altogether. Barbara Grutter, who is white, claimed the University of Michigan Law School denied her admission because of her race.

But Justice Sandra Day O'Connor rescued affirmative action from oblivion with a 5–4 ruling that affirmed Justice Powell's view in *Bakke* that achieving greater diversity was a valid reason for universities to consider race as a factor in admissions. O'Connor expressed hope that within twenty-five years, such programs would no longer be needed. Mirroring the Powell compromise in *Bakke*, O'Connor was the swing vote in striking down another University of Michigan affirmative action program because it seemed too much like a quota system.

The arrival of two more conservative justices in 2005 and 2006, John Roberts Jr. and Samuel Alito Jr., raised hopes among affirmative action opponents that the end to these policies would come sooner than O'Connor's twenty-five-year deadline.

In his first opinion on the subject in 2007, Roberts struck down a public school policy that used race in determining which schools students should attend. "The way to stop discrimination on the basis of race is to stop discriminating on the basis of race," the chief justice wrote.

But in 2016 the court again upheld affirmative action as a way to achieve the valid goal of diversity. In a 4–3 decision in *Fisher v. University of Texas*, Justice Anthony Kennedy—a consistent opponent of affirmative action—changed his mind and said universities deserve deference in devising programs to reach the goal. Affirmative action lives on.

DECISION OF THE COURT
BY JUSTICE LEWIS POWELL JR.

"The special admissions program is undeniably a classification based on race and ethnic background. To the extent that there existed a pool of at least minimally qualified minority applicants to fill the 16 special admissions seats, white applicants could compete only for 84 seats in the entering class, rather than the 100 open to minority applicants. Whether this limitation is described as a quota or a goal, it is a line drawn on the basis of race and ethnic status. . . .

"Petitioner urges us to adopt for the first time a more restrictive view of the Equal Protection Clause, and hold that discrimination against members of the white 'majority' cannot be suspect if its purpose can be characterized as 'benign.' The clock of our liberties, however, cannot be turned back to 1868. It is far too late to argue that the guarantee of equal protection to all persons permits the recognition of special wards entitled to a degree of protection greater than that accorded others. . . .

"Preferential programs may only reinforce common stereotypes holding that certain groups are unable to achieve success without special protection based on a factor having no relationship to individual worth. . . . [T]here is a measure of inequity in forcing innocent persons in respondent's position to bear the burdens of redressing grievances not of their making. . . .

"The fourth goal asserted by petitioner is the attainment of a diverse student body. This clearly is a constitutionally permissible goal for an institution of higher education. Academic freedom, though not a specifically enumerated constitutional right, long has been viewed as a special concern of the First Amendment. The freedom of a university to make its own judgments as to education includes the selection of its student body. . . .

"The fatal flaw in petitioner's preferential program is its disregard of individual rights as guaranteed by the Fourteenth Amendment. Such rights are not absolute. But when a State's distribution of benefits or imposition of burdens hinges on ancestry or the color of a person's skin, that individual is entitled to a demonstration that the challenged classification is necessary to promote a substantial state interest. Petitioner has failed to carry this burden. For this reason, that portion of the California court's judgment holding petitioner's special admissions program invalid under the Fourteenth Amendment must be affirmed."

CONCURRING AND DISSENTING OPINION
BY JUSTICE WILLIAM BRENNAN JR.

"The Court today, in reversing in part the judgment of the Supreme Court of California, affirms the constitutional power of Federal and State Governments to act affirmatively to achieve equal opportunity for all. The difficulty of the issue presented—whether government may use race-conscious programs to redress the continuing effects of past discrimination—and the mature consideration which each of our Brethren has brought to it have resulted in many opinions, no single one speaking for the Court. But this should not and must not mask the central meaning of today's opinions: Government may take race into account when it acts not to demean or insult any racial group, but to remedy disadvantages cast on minorities by past racial prejudice, at least when appropriate findings have been made by judicial, legislative, or administrative bodies with competence to act in this area.

"The chief justice and our brothers Stewart, Rehnquist, and Stevens, have concluded that Title VI of the Civil Rights Act of 1964, prohibits programs such as that at the Davis Medical School. On this statutory theory alone, they would hold that respondent Allan Bakke's rights have been violated, and that he must, therefore, be admitted to the Medical School. Our Brother Powell, reaching the Constitution, concludes that, although race may be taken into account in university admissions, the particular special admissions program used by petitioner, which resulted in the exclusion of respondent Bakke, was not shown to be necessary to achieve petitioner's stated goals. Accordingly, these Members of the Court form a majority of five affirming the judgment of the Supreme Court of California insofar as it holds that respondent Bakke 'is entitled to an order that he be admitted to the University.'

". . . Mr. Justice Powell agrees that some uses of race in university admissions are permissible and, therefore, he joins with us to make five votes reversing the judgment below insofar as it prohibits the University from establishing race-conscious programs in the future."

SEPARATE OPINION BY JUSTICE BYRON WHITE

"I write separately concerning the question of whether Title VI of the Civil Rights Act of 1964 provides for a private cause of action. Four Justices are apparently of the view that such a private cause of action exists, and four Justices assume it for purposes of this case. I am unwilling merely to assume an affirmative answer. If, in fact, no private cause of action exists, this Court and the lower courts as well are without jurisdiction to consider respondent's Title VI claim. As I see it, if we are not obliged to do so, it is at least advisable to address this threshold jurisdictional issue."

SEPARATE OPINION
BY JUSTICE THURGOOD MARSHALL

"I agree with the judgment of the Court only insofar as it permits a university to consider the race of an applicant in making admissions decisions. I do not agree that petitioner's admissions program violates the Constitution. For it must be remembered that, during most of the past 200 years, the Constitution, as interpreted by this Court, did not prohibit the most ingenious and pervasive forms of discrimination against the Negro. Now, when a State acts to remedy the effects of that legacy of discrimination, I cannot believe that this same Constitution stands as a barrier. . . .

"The status of the Negro as property was officially erased by his emancipation at the end of the Civil War. But the long-awaited emancipation, while freeing the Negro from slavery, did not bring him citizenship or equality in any meaningful way. Slavery was replaced by a system of laws which imposed upon the colored race onerous disabilities and burdens, and curtailed their rights in the pursuit of life, liberty, and property to such an extent that their freedom was of little value. . . .

"The position of the Negro today in America is the tragic but inevitable consequence of centuries of unequal treatment. Measured by any benchmark of comfort or achievement, meaningful equality remains a distant dream for the Negro.

"A Negro child today has a life expectancy which is shorter by more than five years than that of a white child. The Negro child's mother is over three times more likely to die of complications in child-birth, and the infant mortality rate for Negroes is nearly twice that for whites. The median income of the Negro family is only 60% that of the median of a white family, and the percentage of Negroes who live in families with incomes below the poverty line is nearly four times greater than that of whites.

"I do not believe that the Fourteenth Amendment requires us to accept that fate. Neither its history nor our past cases lend any support to the conclusion that a university may not remedy the cumulative effects of society's discrimination by giving consideration to race in an effort to increase the number and percentage of Negro doctors."

SEPARATE OPINION BY JUSTICE HARRY BLACKMUN

"At least until the early 1970's, apparently only a very small number, less than 2%, of the physicians, attorneys, and medical and law students in the United States were members of what we now refer to as minority groups. In addition, approximately three-fourths of our Negro physicians were trained at only two medical schools. If ways are not found to remedy that situation, the country can never achieve its professed goal of a society that is not race-conscious.

"I yield to no one in my earnest hope that the time will come when an 'affirmative action' program is unnecessary and is, in truth, only a relic of the past. I would hope that we could reach this stage within a decade, at the most. But the story of *Brown v. Board of Education*, decided almost a quarter of a century ago, suggests that that hope is a slim one. . . .

"It is somewhat ironic to have us so deeply disturbed over a program where race is an element of consciousness, and yet to be aware of the fact, as we are, that institutions of higher learning, albeit more on the undergraduate than the graduate level, have given conceded preferences up to a point to those possessed of athletic skills, to the children of alumni, to the affluent who may bestow their largess on the institutions, and to those having connections with celebrities, the famous, and the powerful.

"Programs of admission to institutions of higher learning are basically a responsibility for academicians and for administrators and the specialists they employ. The judiciary, in contrast, is ill-equipped and poorly trained for this. The administration and management of educational institutions are beyond the competence of judges and are within the special competence of educators, provided always that the educators perform within legal and constitutional bounds. For me, therefore, interference by the judiciary must be the rare exception, and not the rule."

CONCURRING AND DISSENTING OPINION
BY JUSTICE JOHN PAUL STEVENS

"Both petitioner and respondent have asked us to determine the legality of the University's special admissions program by reference to the Constitution. Our settled practice, however, is to avoid the decision of a constitutional issue if a case can be fairly decided on a statutory ground. 'If there is one doctrine more deeply rooted than any other in the process of constitutional adjudication, it is that we ought not to pass on questions of constitutionality . . . unless such adjudication is unavoidable.' The more important the issue, the more force there is to this doctrine. In this case, we are presented with a constitutional question of undoubted and unusual importance. . . .

"Section 601 of the Civil Rights Act of 1964 provides: 'No person in the United States shall, on the ground of race, color, or national origin, be excluded from participation in, be denied the benefits of, or be subjected to discrimination under any program or activity receiving Federal financial assistance.' The University, through its special admissions policy, excluded Bakke from participation in its program of medical education because of his race. The University also acknowledges that it was, and still is, receiving federal financial assistance. The plain language of the statute therefore requires affirmance of the judgment below."

★ ★ ★

UNITED STATES
v. VIRGINIA

– 1996 –

★ **GENDER DISCRIMINATION** ★

By putting an end to male-only admissions at the state-funded Virginia Military Institute, the Supreme Court established that only an "exceedingly persuasive justification" can make a government gender-based distinction constitutional under the Fourteenth Amendment.

ven as the fight for women's rights grew in the last half of the twentieth century, the state-funded Virginia Military Institute in Lexington, Virginia, steadfastly held on to a male-only admissions policy.

The institute defended its "adversative method" of learning, in which new students were tested through harsh treatment by upperclassmen. Freshmen were tormented on the so-called "rat line," and they experienced a total lack of privacy—even in bathrooms. The VMI ethos generated intense loyalty to the school among alumni.

When female applicants were turned away, the U.S. Department of Justice stepped in and sued Virginia, claiming the male-only policy violated the Equal Protection Clause of the Fourteenth Amendment. An appeals court agreed, but gave the state the opportunity to remedy the situation by admitting women, creating a parallel program for women, or ending state support altogether.

In response VMI created the Virginia Women's Institute for Leadership at Mary Baldwin College, a private women's college in Staunton, Virginia. The program was significantly different and less vigorous than VMI's program, offering fewer degree programs and less rigorous training. The new program was approved by lower courts, but the Justice Department went to the Supreme Court to argue that Virginia's different treatment of men and women was still unconstitutional.

The high court was receptive to the government's argument, having come a long way toward striking down most laws and government actions that discriminated between males and females. In *Reed v. Reed*, a 1971 decision, the court for the first time struck down a law because it discriminated against women. The Idaho law gave men an advantage over women in administering estates when a relative died without leaving a will. But even after that ruling, the court did not apply the same high level of "strict scrutiny" to gender discrimination that it used to strike down racial discrimination, perhaps because, unlike with race, there are some undeniable differences between women and men—childbirth, for example—that could, in rare instances, justify different treatment.

Justice Ruth Bader Ginsburg, who had been a prominent women's rights attorney before becoming a judge, wrote the majority opinion. She rejected VMI's argument that its "adversative" training would have to be drastically changed if women were admitted. While some changes would be necessary, the court said they did not amount to an "exceedingly persuasive" reason for preserving the all-male policy.

The court also stated that Virginia's alternative program for women was a "pale shadow" of VMI's. The opinion invoked the 1950 Supreme Court decision in *Sweatt v. Painter*, in which the court said a hastily created law school for African-Americans did not make it constitutional for the University of Texas to keep blacks from attending its long-established law school.

Chief Justice William Rehnquist wrote a concurrence, agreeing with Ginsburg's conclusion that the VMI policy was unconstitutional, but asserting that other alternatives could cure the violation. Justice Antonin Scalia wrote a solitary dissent, stating that it should not be the job of courts to put an end to single-sex education. Justice Clarence Thomas recused himself because his son Jamal was a cadet at VMI during the litigation.

VMI officials were disappointed by the ruling, but over time worked to make the changes necessary for it to admit women. The institute spent $5 million for renovation and the hiring of new personnel, though the tough training practices remained. Over the years since the decision, the number of female students has been relatively low, but the controversy has faded.

DECISION OF THE COURT
BY JUSTICE RUTH BADER GINSBURG

"In 1971, for the first time in our Nation's history, this Court ruled in favor of a woman who complained that her State had denied her the equal protection of its laws [in] *Reed v. Reed*. Since *Reed*, the Court has repeatedly recognized that neither federal nor state government acts compatibly with the equal protection principle when a law or official policy denies to women, simply because they are women, full citizenship stature—equal opportunity to aspire, achieve, participate in and contribute to society based on their individual talents and capacities.

"'Inherent differences' between men and women, we have come to appreciate, remain cause for celebration, but not for denigration of the members of either sex or for artificial constraints on an individual's opportunity. Sex classifications may be used to compensate women 'for particular economic disabilities [they have] suffered' . . . to 'promot[e] equal employment opportunity,' . . . to advance full development of the talent and capacities of our Nation's people. But such classifications may not be used, as they once were, to create or perpetuate the legal, social, and economic inferiority of women.

"Measuring the record in this case against the review standard just described, we conclude that Virginia has shown no 'exceedingly persuasive justification' for excluding all women from the citizen soldier training afforded by VMI. We therefore affirm the Fourth Circuit's initial judgment, which held that Virginia had violated the Fourteenth Amendment's Equal Protection Clause. Because the remedy proffered by Virginia—the Mary Baldwin VWIL program—does not cure the constitutional violation, *i.e.*, it does not provide equal opportunity, we reverse the Fourth Circuit's final judgment in this case. . . .

"Education, to be sure, is not a 'one size fits all' business. The issue, however, is not whether women—or men—should be forced to attend VMI; rather, the question is whether the State can constitutionally deny to women who have the will and capacity, the training and attendant opportunities that VMI uniquely affords.

"The notion that admission of women would downgrade VMI's stature, destroy the adversative system and, with it, even the school, is a judgment hardly proved, a prediction hardly different from other 'self-fulfilling prophec[ies],' once routinely used to deny rights or opportunities. . . .

"Single sex education affords pedagogical benefits to at least some students, Virginia emphasizes, and that reality is uncontested in this litigation. Similarly, it is not disputed that diversity among public educational institutions can serve the public good. But Virginia has not shown that VMI was established, or has been maintained, with a view to diversifying, by its categorical exclusion of women, educational opportunities within the State. In cases of this genre, our precedent instructs that 'benign' justifications proffered in defense of categorical exclusions will not be accepted automatically; a tenable justification must describe actual state purposes, not rationalizations for actions in fact differently grounded.

". . . The constitutional violation in this case is the categorical exclusion of women from an extraordinary educational opportunity afforded men. A proper remedy for an unconstitutional exclusion, we have explained, aims to 'eliminate [so far as possible] the discriminatory effects of the past' and to 'bar like discrimination in the future.'

"Virginia chose not to eliminate, but to leave untouched, VMI's exclusionary policy. For women only, however, Virginia proposed a separate program, different in kind from VMI and unequal in tangible and intangible facilities. . . .

"In myriad respects other than military training, VWIL does not qualify as VMI's equal. VWIL's student body, faculty, course offerings, and facilities hardly match VMI's. Nor can the VWIL graduate anticipate the benefits associated with VMI's 157-year history, the school's prestige, and its influential alumni network.

"Mary Baldwin College, whose degree VWIL students will gain, enrolls first year women with an average combined SAT score about 100 points lower than the average score for VMI freshmen. The Mary Baldwin faculty holds 'significantly fewer Ph.D.'s,' and receives substantially lower salaries, than the faculty at VMI. . . .

"Virginia, in sum, while maintaining VMI for men only, has failed to provide any comparable single-gender women's institution. Instead, the Commonwealth has created a VWIL program fairly appraised as a 'pale shadow' of VMI in terms of the range of curricular choices and faculty stature, funding, prestige, alumni support and influence."

CONCURRING OPINION
BY CHIEF JUSTICE WILLIAM REHNQUIST

"The Court holds first that Virginia violates the Equal Protection Clause by maintaining the Virginia Military Institute's (VMI's) all male admissions policy, and second that establishing the Virginia Women's Institute for Leadership (VWIL) program does not remedy that violation. While I agree with these conclusions, I disagree with the Court's analysis and so I write separately. . . .

"The Court defines the constitutional violation in this case as 'the categorical exclusion of women from an extraordinary educational opportunity afforded to men.' By defining the violation in this way, and by emphasizing that a remedy for a constitutional violation must place the victims of discrimination in 'the position they would have occupied in the absence of [discrimination],' *ibid.*, the Court necessarily implies that the only adequate remedy would be the admission of women to the all-male institution. As the foregoing discussion suggests, I would not define the violation in this way; it is not the 'exclusion of women' that violates the Equal Protection Clause, but the maintenance of an all men school without providing any—much less a comparable—institution for women.

"Accordingly, the remedy should not necessarily require either the admission of women to VMI, or the creation of a VMI clone for women. An adequate remedy in my opinion might be a demonstration by Virginia that its interest in educating men in a single sex environment is matched by its interest in educating women in a single sex institution. To demonstrate such, the State does not need to create two institutions with the same number of faculty PhD's, similar SAT scores, or comparable athletic fields. Nor would it necessarily require that the women's institution offer the same curriculum as the men's; one could be strong in computer science, the other could be strong in liberal arts. It would be a sufficient remedy, I think, if the two institutions offered the same quality of education and were of the same overall calibre."

DISSENTING OPINION BY JUSTICE ANTONIN SCALIA

"Much of the Court's opinion is devoted to deprecating the closed mindedness of our forebears with regard to women's education, and even with regard to the treatment of women in areas that have nothing to do with education. Closed minded they were—as every age is, including our own, with regard to matters it cannot guess, because it simply does not consider them debatable. The virtue of a democratic system with a First Amendment is that it readily enables the people, over time, to be persuaded that what they took for granted is not so, and to change their laws accordingly. That system is destroyed if the smug assurances of each age are removed from the democratic process and written into the Constitution. So to counterbalance the Court's criticism of our ancestors, let me say a word in their praise: they left us free to change. The same cannot be said of this most illiberal Court, which has embarked on a course of inscribing one after another of the current preferences of the society (and in some cases only the counter majoritarian preferences of the society's law-trained elite) into our Basic Law. Today it enshrines the notion that no substantial educational value is to be served by an all men's military academy—so that the decision by the people of Virginia to maintain such an institution denies equal protection to women who cannot attend that institution but can attend others. Since it is entirely clear that the Constitution of the United States—the old one—takes no sides in this educational debate, I dissent. . . .

"Today, however, change is forced upon Virginia, and reversion to single sex education is prohibited nationwide, not by democratic processes but by order of this Court. Even while bemoaning the sorry, bygone days of 'fixed notions' concerning women's education, the Court favors current notions so fixedly that it is willing to write them into the Constitution of the United States by application of custom built 'tests.' This is not the interpretation of a Constitution, but the creation of one."

* * *

BUSH v. GORE

– 2000 –

★   **VOTING RIGHTS**   ★

In an unprecedented sequence of events, the Supreme Court in effect decided the outcome of the 2000 presidential election in favor of George W. Bush by halting the recount of ballots in certain Florida counties. Its 5–4 decision ruled that the different standards being used for the recount violated the Equal Protection Clause of the Fourteenth Amendment.

Supreme Court prides itself on operating above and apart from the political fray. But in the cascade of events that made the 2000 election unique in American history, avoiding politics proved impossible.

As Election Day drew near, the race between Republican George W. Bush and Democrat Al Gore became extremely close, according to polls.

Early on election night, it appeared that Gore would win nationally because he was winning Florida, a key state with twenty-five Electoral College votes. But the tide shifted when networks predicted that Bush would win Florida, and Gore was ready to concede the election. At the last minute Gore decided not to concede, launching a five-week period in which the public was not at all certain who would be the next president.

An automatic recount in Florida did not resolve things, at one point showing that only 229 votes separated the candidates among nearly six million votes cast. Inevitably, the battle moved to the courts, and lawyers for both sides descended on Florida—including John Roberts Jr., who would later become chief justice of the United States, and R. Ted Cruz, who became a presidential candidate in 2016.

The litigation was fueled by reports of ballot irregularities that confused voters and may have skewed the results.

Democrats pushed for a manual recount in several counties, while Republicans wanted nothing of the kind, asserting that Bush had already won. Republicans went to federal court to stop the recount, but the judge said the dispute belonged in Florida courts. On November 20, the Florida Supreme Court ruled that the recounts could continue through Thanksgiving weekend.

Republicans took the case to the U.S. Supreme Court, challenging the validity of the recounts based on the Fourteenth Amendment. On November 24, the day after Thanksgiving, the high court announced it would consider the case a week later.

The Supreme Court sent the case back to the Florida Supreme Court, which responded in an unexpected way. On December 8, it ordered recounts to resume statewide under a state law allowing for such recounts. Bush lawyers immediately appealed the decision, and the next day the U.S. Supreme Court issued an injunction halting the recounts pending its own evaluation.

The injunction placed the Supreme Court at center stage in the ongoing election controversy. Ordinarily a quiet place, the court was surrounded by hundreds of demonstrators, many of them shouting at each other. Responding to requests from the public, the court agreed to release the audiotapes of the oral arguments immediately after they ended.

With unprecedented speed, the court issued its historic ruling the following day. It issued an unsigned or "per curiam" opinion. Justices John Paul Stevens, David Souter, Ruth Bader Ginsburg, and Stephen Breyer dissented, which meant in effect that Chief Justice William Rehnquist and Justices Sandra Day O'Connor, Antonin Scalia, Anthony Kennedy, and Clarence Thomas agreed with the unsigned ruling.

The majority invoked the Fourteenth Amendment's guarantee of equal protection of the laws and the principle of "one person one vote" to rule that the recounts ordered by the Florida Supreme Court were improper and should be halted.

Even though there were four dissenting justices, seven of the nine justices found that the recount posed constitutional problems. Dissents by Justices David Souter and Stephen Breyer acknowledged equal protection concerns. But all four of the dissenting justices sharply criticized the majority for concluding that there was no time left for the recounts to take place.

The court's decision was extremely controversial, but it had the immediate effect of ending the turmoil of the 2000 election. The next day Vice President Gore conceded the election, stating that "while I strongly disagree with the court's decision, I accept it." He was praised for placing the rule of law and respect for the Supreme Court above his own interests.

For years after the ruling, when Justice Antonin Scalia was asked about *Bush v. Gore*, his answer was, "Get over it." Most Americans did just that, though it still rankled many who viewed the decision as result-oriented and political. A conservative majority that usually deferred to state courts interpreting their own laws had done the opposite by ordering the recounts to end. Many wondered if the court would have ruled the same way if it had been the Republican Bush who wanted the recounts to continue, and the Democrat Gore was the one opposing them.

UNSIGNED DECISION OF THE COURT

"Our consideration is limited to the present circumstances, for the problem of equal protection in election processes generally presents many complexities.

"The question before the Court is not whether local entities, in the exercise of their expertise, may develop different systems for implementing elections. Instead, we are presented with a situation where a state court with the power to assure uniformity has ordered a statewide recount with minimal procedural safeguards. When a court orders a statewide remedy, there must be at least some assurance that the rudimentary requirements of equal treatment and fundamental fairness are satisfied. . . .

"Upon due consideration of the difficulties identified to this point, it is obvious that the recount cannot be conducted in compliance with the requirements of equal protection and due process without substantial additional work. It would require not only the adoption (after opportunity for argument) of adequate statewide standards for determining what is a legal vote, and practicable procedures to implement them, but also orderly judicial review of any disputed matters that might arise. . . .

"The Supreme Court of Florida has said that the legislature intended the State's electors to 'participat[e] fully in the federal electoral process.' That statute, in turn, requires that any controversy or contest that is designed to lead to a conclusive selection of electors be completed by December 12. That date is upon us, and there is no recount procedure in place under the State Supreme Court's order that comports with minimal constitutional standards. Because it is evident that any recount seeking to meet the December 12 date will be unconstitutional for the reasons we have discussed, we reverse the judgment of the Supreme Court of Florida ordering a recount to proceed. . . .

"None are more conscious of the vital limits on judicial authority than are the members of this Court, and none stand more in admiration of the Constitution's design to leave the selection of the President to the people, through their legislatures, and to the political sphere. When contending parties invoke the process of the courts, however, it becomes our unsought responsibility to resolve the federal and constitutional issues the judicial system has been forced to confront."

CONCURRING OPINION
BY CHIEF JUSTICE WILLIAM REHNQUIST

"We deal here not with an ordinary election, but with an election for the President of the United States. In *Burroughs v. United States*, we said: 'While presidential electors are not officers or agents of the federal government, they exercise federal functions under, and discharge duties in virtue of authority conferred by, the Constitution of the United States. The President is vested with the executive power of the nation. The importance of his election and the vital character of its relationship to and effect upon the welfare and safety of the whole people cannot be too strongly stated'. . . .

"In most cases, comity and respect for federalism compel us to defer to the decisions of state courts on issues of state law. That practice reflects our understanding that the decisions of state courts are definitive pronouncements of the will of the States as sovereigns. Of course, in ordinary cases, the distribution of powers among the branches of a State's government raises no questions of federal constitutional law, subject to the requirement that the government be republican in character. But there are a few exceptional cases in which the Constitution imposes a duty or confers a power on a particular branch of a State's government. This is one of them."

DISSENTING OPINION
BY JUSTICE JOHN PAUL STEVENS

"The Constitution assigns to the States the primary responsibility for determining the manner of selecting the Presidential electors. When questions arise about the meaning of state laws, including election laws, it is our settled practice to accept the opinions of the highest courts of the States as providing the final answers. On rare occasions, however, either federal statutes or the Federal Constitution may require federal judicial intervention in state elections. This is not such an occasion. . . .

"What must underlie petitioners' entire federal assault on the Florida election procedures is an unstated lack of confidence in the impartiality and capacity of the state judges who would make the critical decisions if the vote count were to proceed. Otherwise, their position is wholly without merit. The endorsement of that position by the majority of this Court can only lend credence to the most cynical appraisal of the work of judges throughout the land. It is confidence in the men and women who administer the judicial system that is the true backbone of the rule of law. Time will one day heal the wound to that confidence that will be inflicted by today's decision. One thing, however, is certain. Although we may never know with complete certainty the identity of the winner of this year's Presidential election, the identity of the loser is perfectly clear. It is the Nation's confidence in the judge as an impartial guardian of the rule of law."

DISSENTING OPINION BY JUSTICE DAVID SOUTER

"The Court should not have reviewed either *Bush v. Palm Beach County Canvassing Bd.*, or this case, and should not have stopped Florida's attempt to recount all undervote ballots by issuing a stay of the Florida Supreme Court's orders during the period of this review. If this Court had allowed the State to follow the course indicated by the opinions of its own Supreme Court, it is entirely possible that there would ultimately have been no issue requiring our review, and political tension could have worked itself out in the Congress following the procedure provided in 3 U.S.C. § 15. The case being before us, however, its resolution by the majority is another erroneous decision. . . .

"In deciding what to do about this, we should take account of the fact that electoral votes are due to be cast in six days. I would therefore remand the case to the courts of Florida with instructions to establish uniform standards for evaluating the several types of ballots that have prompted differing treatments, to be applied within and among counties when passing on such identical ballots in any further recounting (or successive recounting) that the courts might order.

"Unlike the majority, I see no warrant for this Court to assume that Florida could not possibly comply with this requirement before the date set for the meeting of electors, December 18. . . . But as Justice Breyer has pointed out, no showing has been made of legal overvotes uncounted, and counsel for Gore made an uncontradicted representation to the Court that the statewide total of undervotes is about 60,000. To recount these manually would be a tall order, but before this Court stayed the effort to do that the courts of Florida were ready to do their best to get that job done. There is no justification for denying the State the opportunity to try to count all disputed ballots now."

DISSENTING OPINION
BY JUSTICE RUTH BADER GINSBURG

"The Chief Justice acknowledges that provisions of Florida's Election Code 'may well admit of more than one interpretation.' But instead of respecting the state high court's province to say what the State's Election Code means, the Chief Justice maintains that Florida's Supreme Court has veered so far from the ordinary practice of judicial review that what it did cannot properly be called judging.

My colleagues have offered a reasonable construction of Florida's law. Their construction coincides with the view of one of Florida's seven Supreme Court justices. I might join the Chief Justice were it my commission to interpret Florida law. But disagreement with the Florida court's interpretation of its own State's law does not warrant the conclusion that the justices of that court have legislated. There is no cause here to believe that the members of Florida's high court have done less than 'their mortal best to discharge their oath of office,' and no cause to upset their reasoned interpretation of Florida law."

DISSENTING OPINION BY JUSTICE STEPHEN BREYER

"In this highly politicized matter, the appearance of a split decision runs the risk of undermining the public's confidence in the Court itself. That confidence is a public treasure. It has been built slowly over many years, some of which were marked by a Civil War and the tragedy of segregation. It is a vitally necessary ingredient of any successful effort to protect basic liberty and, indeed, the rule of law itself. We run no risk of returning to the days when a President (responding to this Court's efforts to protect the Cherokee Indians) might have said, 'John Marshall has made his decision; now let him enforce it!'. . . . But we do risk a self-inflicted wound—a wound that may harm not just the Court, but the Nation.

"I fear that in order to bring this agonizingly long election process to a definitive conclusion, we have not adequately attended to that necessary 'check upon our own exercise of power,' 'our own sense of self-restraint.' Justice Brandeis once said of the Court, "The most important thing we do is not doing." What it does today, the Court should have left undone. I would repair the damage done as best we now can, by permitting the Florida recount to continue under uniform standards."

★ ★ ★

DISTRICT OF COLUMBIA
v. HELLER

– 2008 –

★   RIGHT TO BEAR ARMS   ★

Ending a long-running debate, the Supreme Court declared that the Second Amendment provides for an individual right to buy and possess firearms, a right that is not limited to the arming of state militias.

The oddly phrased, comma-filled wording of the Second Amendment has confounded legal scholars for a long time: "A well regulated Militia, being necessary to the security of a free State, the right of the people to keep and bear arms, shall not be infringed."

Did its reference to a "well-regulated militia" mean that the right to bear arms only refers to members of long-ago state militias? Or was that just a throat-clearing preface that does nothing to limit "the right of the people" in general to possess firearms?

In spite of the sharp disagreement over the meaning of the Second Amendment, the Supreme Court did not appear to be in any hurry to resolve the dispute. The only pronouncement it made on the subject in the twentieth century came in the 1939 case *Miller v. United States*, which declared that the "obvious purpose" of the amendment was to arm militias, not individuals.

Challenges aimed at overturning that interpretation fell flat until the beginning of the twenty-first century, when more conservatives joined the court. Gun-rights advocates saw an opportunity to turn the Second Amendment from an archaic provision into a proclamation of an individual right to own firearms.

A group of libertarians mounted the challenge, representing several Washington, D.C., residents who said the district's strict handgun ordinances violated the Second Amendment. As the case proceeded through lower courts, only Dick Heller, a federal employee who had been denied a gun permit, remained as a plaintiff.

Justice Antonin Scalia, the leader of the court's conservative wing, wrote the court's 5–4 majority opinion. An advocate of interpreting the Constitution by its original meaning, he delved deeply into the meaning of the words of the Second Amendment and concluded that "they guarantee the individual right to possess and carry weapons in case of confrontation."

"This is a great moment in American history," said Wayne LaPierre, vice president of the National Rifle Association, in response to the decision.

Perhaps demonstrating the flaws of originalism—using original sources and texts to interpret the Constitution—dissenting justice John Paul Stevens used the same approach of examining texts from the founding of the Constitution to reach the opposite conclusion—that the Second Amendment was only about arming militia members.

Justice Stephen Breyer also wrote a dissent, emphasizing that the Second Amendment's protection of gun rights is not absolute, and asserting that the D.C. ordinance was neither unreasonable nor inappropriate. Justices Stevens, David Souter, and Ruth Bader Ginsburg joined Breyer.

But because the *Heller* decision applied only to the laws of the District of Columbia, a federal enclave, it took another case—*McDonald v. Chicago*—to apply the *Heller* decision to state laws governing gun use across the nation. That 2010 ruling declared that the "individual right" view of the Second Amendment applied to state laws as well.

But the *Heller* and *McDonald* decisions did not end the debate over gun control—a debate that often comes into public view after a mass shooting. Some gun-control measures have been upheld, partly because of this section of Scalia's ruling that stated:

"Nothing in our opinion should be taken to cast doubt on longstanding prohibitions on the possession of firearms by felons and the mentally ill, or laws forbidding the carrying of firearms in sensitive places such as schools and government buildings, or laws imposing conditions and qualifications on the commercial sale of arms."

DECISION OF THE COURT
BY JUSTICE ANTONIN SCALIA

"The Second Amendment provides: 'A well-regulated Militia, being necessary to the security of a free State, the right of the people to keep and bear Arms, shall not be infringed.' In interpreting this text, we are guided by the principle that '[t]he Constitution was written to be understood by the voters; its words and phrases were used in their normal and ordinary as distinguished from technical meaning.' Normal meaning may of course include an idiomatic meaning, but it excludes secret or technical meanings that would not have been known to ordinary citizens in the founding generation.

"The two sides in this case have set out very different interpretations of the Amendment. Petitioners and today's dissenting Justices believe that it protects only the right to possess and carry a firearm in connection with militia service. Respondent argues that it protects an individual right to possess a firearm unconnected with service in a militia, and to use that arm for traditionally lawful purposes, such as self-defense within the home.

"The Second Amendment is naturally divided into two parts: its prefatory clause and its operative clause. The former does not limit the latter grammatically, but rather announces a purpose. The Amendment could be rephrased, 'Because a well-regulated Militia is necessary to the security of a free State, the right of the people to keep and bear Arms shall not be infringed.' Although this structure of the Second Amendment is unique in our Constitution, other legal documents of the founding era, particularly individual-rights provisions of state constitutions, commonly included a prefatory statement of purpose. . . .

". . . Nowhere else in the Constitution does a 'right' attributed to 'the people' refer to anything other than an individual right. . . .

"'[T]he people,' refers to all members of the political community, not an unspecified subset. . . .

"We start therefore with a strong presumption that the Second Amendment right is exercised individually and belongs to all Americans. . . .

"At the time of the founding, as now, to 'bear' meant to 'carry'. . . . When used with 'arms,' however, the term has a meaning that refers to carrying for a particular purpose—confrontation. . . . Although the phrase implies that the carrying of the weapon is for the purpose of 'offensive or defensive action,' it in no way connotes participation in a structured military organization.

"Putting all of these textual elements together, we find that they guarantee the individual right to possess and carry weapons in case of confrontation.

"There seems to us no doubt, on the basis of both text and history, that the Second Amendment conferred an individual right to keep and bear arms. Of course the right was not unlimited, just as the First Amendment's right of free speech was not. . . .

". . . It should be unsurprising that such a significant matter has been for so long judicially unresolved. For most of our history, the Bill of Rights was not thought applicable to the States, and the Federal Government did not significantly regulate the possession of firearms by law-abiding citizens. Other provisions of the Bill of Rights have similarly remained unilluminated for lengthy periods. This Court first held a law to violate the First Amendment's guarantee of freedom of speech in 1931, almost 150 years after the Amendment was ratified. . . .

". . . Although we do not undertake an exhaustive historical analysis today of the full scope of the Second Amendment, nothing in our opinion should be taken to cast doubt on longstanding prohibitions on the possession of firearms by felons and the mentally ill, or laws forbidding the carrying of firearms in sensitive places such as schools and government buildings, or laws imposing conditions and qualifications on the commercial sale of arms.

"We also recognize another important limitation on the right to keep and carry arms. *Miller* said, as we have explained, that the sorts of weapons protected were those 'in common use at the time.' We think that limitation is fairly supported by the historical tradition of prohibiting the carrying of 'dangerous and unusual weapons'. . . .

"In sum, we hold that the District's ban on handgun possession in the home violates the Second Amendment, as does its prohibition against rendering any lawful firearm in the home operable for the purpose of immediate self-defense. Assuming that Heller is not disqualified from the exercise of Second Amendment rights, the District must permit him to register his handgun and must issue him a license to carry it in the home.

". . . Undoubtedly some think that the Second Amendment is outmoded in a society where our standing army is the pride of our Nation, where well-trained police forces provide personal security, and where gun violence is a serious problem. That is perhaps debatable, but what is not debatable is that it is not the role of this Court to pronounce the Second Amendment extinct."

DISSENTING OPINION
BY JUSTICE JOHN PAUL STEVENS

"The question presented by this case is not whether the Second Amendment protects a 'collective right' or an 'individual right.' Surely it protects a right that can be enforced by individuals. But a conclusion that the Second Amendment protects an individual right does not tell us anything about the scope of that right.

"Guns are used to hunt, for self-defense, to commit crimes, for sporting activities, and to perform military duties. The Second Amendment plainly does not protect the right to use a gun to rob a bank; it is equally clear that it does encompass the right to use weapons for certain military purposes. Whether it also protects the right to possess and use guns for nonmilitary purposes like hunting and personal self-defense is the question presented by this case. The text of the Amendment, its history, and our decision in *United States v. Miller*, provide a clear answer to that question.

"The Second Amendment was adopted to protect the right of the people of each of the several States to maintain a well-regulated militia. It was a response to concerns raised during the ratification of the Constitution that the power of Congress to disarm the state militias and create a national standing army posed an intolerable threat to the sovereignty of the several States. Neither the text of the Amendment nor the arguments advanced by its proponents evidenced the slightest interest in limiting any legislature's authority to regulate private civilian uses of firearms. Specifically, there is no indication that the Framers of the Amendment intended to enshrine the common-law right of self-defense in the Constitution. . . .

". . . The view of the Amendment we took in *Miller*—that it protects the right to keep and bear arms for certain military purposes, but that it does not curtail the Legislature's power to regulate the nonmilitary use and ownership of weapons—is both the most natural reading of the Amendment's text and the interpretation most faithful to the history of its adoption.

"Since our decision in *Miller*, hundreds of judges have relied on the view of the Amendment we endorsed there; we ourselves affirmed it in 1980. No new evidence has surfaced since 1980 supporting the view that the Amendment was intended to curtail the power of Congress to regulate civilian use or misuse of weapons. Indeed, a review of the drafting history of the Amendment demonstrates that its Framers rejected proposals that would have broadened its coverage to include such uses.

"The opinion the Court announces today fails to identify any new evidence supporting the view that the Amendment was intended to limit the power of Congress to regulate civilian uses of weapons. Unable to point to any such evidence, the Court stakes its holding on a strained and unpersuasive reading of the Amendment's text; significantly different provisions in the 1689 English Bill of Rights, and in various 19th-century State Constitutions; post-enactment commentary that was available to the Court when it decided *Miller*; and, ultimately, a feeble attempt to distinguish *Miller* that places more emphasis on the Court's decisional process than on the reasoning in the opinion itself.

"Even if the textual and historical arguments on both sides of the issue were evenly balanced, respect for the well-settled views of all of our predecessors on this Court, and for the rule of law itself would prevent most jurists from endorsing such a dramatic upheaval in the law. As Justice Cardozo observed years ago, the 'labor of judges would be increased almost to the breaking point if every past decision could be reopened in every case, and one could not lay one's own course of bricks on the secure foundation of the courses laid by others who had gone before him.'"

DISSENTING OPINION BY JUSTICE STEPHEN BREYER

"I shall show that the District's law is consistent with the Second Amendment even if that Amendment is interpreted as protecting a wholly separate interest in individual self-defense. That is so because the District's regulation, which focuses upon the presence of handguns in high-crime urban areas, represents a permissible legislative response to a serious, indeed life-threatening, problem.

"Thus I here assume that one objective (but, as the majority concedes, not the primary objective) of those who wrote the Second Amendment was to help assure citizens that they would have arms available for purposes of self-defense. Even so, a legislature could reasonably conclude that the law will advance goals of great public importance, namely, saving lives, preventing injury, and reducing crime. The law is tailored to the urban crime problem in that it is local in scope and thus affects only a geographic area both limited in size and entirely urban; the law concerns handguns, which are specially linked to urban gun deaths and injuries, and which are the overwhelmingly favorite weapon of armed criminals; and at the same time, the law imposes a burden upon gun owners that seems proportionately no greater than restrictions in existence at the time the Second Amendment was adopted. In these circumstances, the District's law falls within the zone that the Second Amendment leaves open to regulation by legislatures. . . .

"Although I adopt for present purposes the majority's position that the Second Amendment embodies a general concern about self-defense, I shall not assume that the Amendment contains a specific untouchable right to keep guns in the house to shoot burglars. The majority, which presents evidence in favor of the former proposition, does not, because it cannot, convincingly show that the Second Amendment seeks to maintain the latter in pristine, unregulated form.

"To the contrary, colonial history itself offers important examples of the kinds of gun regulation that citizens would then have thought compatible with the "right to keep and bear arms," whether embodied in Federal or State Constitutions, or the background common law. And those examples include substantial regulation of firearms in urban areas, including regulations that imposed obstacles to the use of firearms for the protection of the home.

"Boston, Philadelphia, and New York City, the three largest cities in America during that period, all restricted the firing of guns within city limits to at least some degree. . . .

"From 1993 to 1997, there were 180,533 firearm-related deaths in the United States, an average of over 36,000 per year. Fifty-one percent were suicides, 44% were homicides, 1%

were legal interventions, 3% were unintentional accidents, and 1% were of undetermined causes. Over that same period there were an additional 411,800 nonfatal firearm-related injuries treated in U.S. hospitals, an average of over 82,000 per year. Of these, 62% resulted from assaults, 17% were unintentional, 6% were suicide attempts, 1% were legal interventions, and 13% were of unknown causes. . . .

"Handguns are involved in a majority of fire-arm deaths and injuries in the United States. From 1993 to 1997, 81% of firearm-homicide victims were killed by handgun. In the same period, for the 41% of firearm injuries for which the weapon type is known, 82% of them were from handguns. And among children under the age of 20, handguns account for approximately 70% of all unintentional firearm-related injuries and deaths. . . .

"The majority spends the first 54 pages of its opinion attempting to rebut Justice Stevens' evidence that the Amendment was enacted with a purely militia-related purpose. In the majority's view, the Amendment also protects an interest in armed personal self-defense, at least to some degree. But the majority does not tell us precisely what that interest is. 'Putting all of [the Second Amendment's] textual elements together,' the majority says, 'we find that they guarantee the individual right to possess and carry weapons in case of confrontation.' Then, three pages later, it says that 'we do not read the Second Amendment to permit citizens to carry arms for any sort of confrontation.'

Yet, with one critical exception, it does not explain which confrontations count. It simply leaves that question unanswered. . . .

"Nor is it at all clear to me how the majority decides *which* loaded 'arms' a homeowner may keep. The majority says that that Amendment protects those weapons 'typically possessed by law-abiding citizens for lawful purposes.' This definition conveniently excludes machine guns, but permits handguns, which the majority describes as 'the most popular weapon chosen by Americans for self-defense in the home.' But what sense does this approach make? According to the majority's reasoning, if Congress and the States lift restrictions on the possession and use of machine guns, and people buy machine guns to protect their homes, the Court will have to reverse course and find that the Second Amendment does, in fact, protect the individual self-defense-related right to possess a machine gun."

★ ★ ★

CITIZENS UNITED v. FEDERAL ELECTION COMMISSION

– 2010 –

★   CAMPAIGN FINANCE   ★

Making it easier for corporations and unions to influence political campaigns, the Supreme Court, on First Amendment grounds, struck down the law that prohibited such organizations from making independent expenditures advocating the election or defeat of a candidate.

ooting out corruption in American political campaigns has been a goal for reformers for more than a century. In 1907, Congress passed the Tillman Act, which prohibited contributions from corporations to candidates for federal office. That law set a baseline that lasted for decades.

The 1972 Watergate break-in and scandal exposed secret illegal contributions to President

Richard Nixon's re-election campaign and led to more reform measures. In the 1976 *Buckley v. Valeo* decision, the Supreme Court upheld one of those measures that limited contributions for candidates in federal elections. But it struck down a limit on how much money candidates themselves could spend on their campaigns, finding that it violated their freedom of expression.

The ruling did little to stem the flow of money into political campaigns through other pathways such as political action committees. At the same time however, an increasingly conservative Supreme Court began to take a different view of campaign reform laws as violations of the First Amendment because of the restrictions they placed on core political speech during campaigns.

In 2002, Congress passed the Bipartisan Campaign Reform Act, which, among other things, barred corporations and unions from directly financing, within sixty days of an election, so-called "electioneering communications" that mention specific candidates.

The electioneering provision was challenged in 2008 by a conservative nonprofit corporation called Citizens United that wanted to disseminate a documentary that was highly critical of then-presidential candidate Hillary Clinton. A lower court rejected the challenge and the case went before the Supreme Court.

Before the high court, supporters of the law cited a 1990 precedent, *Austin v. Michigan Chamber of Commerce*, which upheld a state law banning corporations from directly supporting or opposing candidates.

But conservative justices were clearly disturbed by the idea of banning the broadcast of a film that criticized a presidential candidate, no matter who funded it. The federal government did not help its own case when its lawyer acknowledged during arguments in March 2009 that under the law, even a book could be banned. "That's pretty incredible," Justice Samuel Alito Jr. said.

When the case was reargued in September 2009, the government said that book-burning would not be allowed, but the damage was done. In January 2010, a 5–4 majority ruled that under the First Amendment, Congress may not bar corporations and unions from using their own money to make independent expenditures to support or oppose candidates for office.

Justice Anthony Kennedy said of the law, "Its purpose and effect are to silence entities whose voices the government deems to be suspect." The majority overturned the *Austin* precedent.

By a separate 8–1 vote, however, the court upheld another provision of the law requiring those backing electioneering communications to disclose their names to the public. Only Justice Clarence Thomas argued that even that provision was unconstitutional.

Dissenting justice John Paul Stevens attacked the majority, stating that "a democracy cannot function effectively when its constituent members believe laws are being bought and sold." Three liberal justices—Ruth Bader Ginsburg, Stephen Breyer, and Sonia Sotomayor—joined Stevens.

In an unusual move, President Barack Obama criticized the ruling during his State of the Union address a few days after the decision was issued. "Last week, the Supreme Court reversed a century of law to open the floodgates for special interests—including foreign corporations—to spend without limit in our elections." Justice Alito, who was attending the address, conspicuously shook his head no and mouthed the words "not true."

The impact of *Citizens United* is still a matter of debate, though it is undeniable that the amount of money that pours into campaigns from corporations and unions has only gotten bigger, including unlimited independent expenditures to "super PACs."

DECISION OF THE COURT
BY JUSTICE ANTHONY KENNEDY

"The First Amendment provides that 'Congress shall make no law. . . abridging the freedom of speech.' Laws enacted to control or suppress speech may operate at different points in the speech process. . . .

"The law before us is an outright ban, backed by criminal sanctions. Section 441b makes it a felony for all corporations—including nonprofit advocacy corporation—either to expressly advocate the election or defeat of candidates or to broadcast electioneering communications within 30 days of a primary election and 60 days of a general election. . . .

"Speech is an essential mechanism of democracy, for it is the means to hold officials accountable to the people. The right of citizens to inquire, to hear, to speak, and to use information to reach consensus is a precondition to enlightened self-government and a necessary means to protect it. The First Amendment '"has its fullest and most urgent application" to speech uttered during a campaign for political office.'

"For these reasons, political speech must prevail against laws that would suppress it, whether by design or inadvertence. Laws that burden political speech are 'subject to strict scrutiny,' which requires the Government to prove that the restriction 'furthers a compelling interest and is narrowly tailored to achieve that interest'. . . .

"Quite apart from the purpose or effect of regulating content, moreover, the Government may commit a constitutional wrong when by law it identifies certain preferred speakers. By taking the right to speak from some and giving it to others, the Government deprives the disadvantaged person or class of the right to use speech to strive to establish worth, standing, and respect for the speaker's voice. The Government may not by these means deprive the public of the right and privilege to determine for itself what speech and speakers are worthy of consideration. The First Amendment protects speech and speaker, and the ideas that flow from each. . . .

"The censorship we now confront is vast in its reach. The Government has 'muffle[d] the voices that best represent the most significant segments of the economy.' And 'the electorate [has been] deprived of information, knowledge and opinion vital to its function.' By suppressing the speech of manifold corporations, both for-profit and non-profit, the Government prevents their voices and viewpoints from reaching the public and advising voters on which persons or entities are hostile to their interests. Factions will necessarily form in our Republic, but the remedy of 'destroying the liberty' of some factions is 'worse than the disease.' Factions should be checked by permitting them all to speak, and by entrusting the people to judge what is true and what is false. . . .

"When Government seeks to use its full power, including the criminal law, to command where a person may get his or her information or what distrusted source he or she may not hear, it uses censorship to control thought. This is unlawful. The First Amendment confirms the freedom to think for ourselves."

CONCURRENCE
BY CHIEF JUSTICE JOHN ROBERTS JR.

"The Government urges us in this case to uphold a direct prohibition on political speech. It asks us to embrace a theory of the First Amendment that would allow censorship not only of television and radio broadcasts, but of pamphlets, posters, the Internet, and virtually any other medium that corporations and unions might find useful in expressing their views on matters of public concern. Its theory, if accepted, would empower the Government to prohibit newspapers from running editorials or opinion pieces supporting or opposing candidates for office, so long as the newspapers were owned by corporations—as the major ones are. First Amendment rights could be confined to individuals, subverting the vibrant public discourse that is at the foundation of our democracy.

"The Court properly rejects that theory, and I join its opinion in full. The First Amendment protects more than just the individual on a soapbox and the lonely pamphleteer. . . .

"We have had two rounds of briefing in this case, two oral arguments, and 54 *amicus* briefs to help us carry out our obligation to decide the necessary constitutional questions according to law. We have also had the benefit of a comprehensive dissent that has helped ensure that the Court has considered all the relevant issues. This careful consideration convinces me that Congress violates the First Amendment when it decrees that some speakers may not engage in political speech at election time, when it matters most."

CONCURRING OPINION
BY JUSTICE ANTONIN SCALIA

"The dissent says that when the Framers 'constitutionalized the right to free speech in the First Amendment, it was the free speech of individual Americans that they had in mind.' That is no doubt true. All the provisions of the Bill of Rights set forth the rights of individual men and women—not, for example, of trees or polar bears. But the individual person's right to speak includes the right to speak in association with other individual persons. Surely the dissent does not believe that speech by the Republican Party or the Democratic Party can be censored because it is not the speech of 'an individual American.' It is the speech of many individual Americans, who have associated in a common cause, giving the leadership of the party the right to speak on their behalf. The association of individuals in a business corporation is no different—or at least it cannot be denied the right to speak on the simplistic ground that it is not 'an individual American.'

"But to return to, and summarize, my principal point, which is the conformity of today's opinion with the original meaning of the First Amendment. The Amendment is written in terms of 'speech,' not speakers. Its text offers no foothold for excluding any category of speaker, from single individuals to partnerships of individuals, to unincorporated associations of individuals, to incorporated associations of individuals—and the dissent offers no evidence about the original meaning of the text to support any such exclusion. We are therefore simply left with the question whether the speech at issue in this case is 'speech' covered by the First Amendment. No one says otherwise. A documentary film critical of a potential Presidential candidate is core political speech, and its nature as such does not change simply because it was funded by a corporation. . . . Indeed, to exclude or impede corporate speech is to muzzle the principal agents of the modern free economy. We should celebrate rather than condemn the addition of this speech to the public debate."

PARTIAL CONCURRING AND DISSENTING OPINION BY JUSTICE JOHN PAUL STEVENS

"The real issue in this case concerns how, not if, the appellant may finance its electioneering. Citizens United is a wealthy nonprofit corporation that runs a political action committee (PAC) with millions of dollars in assets. Under the Bipartisan Campaign Reform Act of 2002 (BCRA), it could have used those assets to televise and promote *Hillary: The Movie* wherever and whenever it wanted to. It also could have spent unrestricted sums to broadcast *Hillary* at any time other than the 30 days before the last primary election. Neither Citizens United's nor any other corporation's speech has been 'banned.' All that the parties dispute is whether Citizens United had a right to use the funds in its general treasury to pay for broadcasts during the 30-day period. The notion that the First Amendment dictates an affirmative answer to that question is, in my judgment, profoundly misguided. . . .

"The basic premise underlying the Court's ruling is its iteration, and constant reiteration, of the proposition that the First Amendment bars regulatory distinctions based on a speaker's identity, including its 'identity' as a corporation. While that glittering generality has rhetorical appeal, it is not a correct statement of the law. Nor does it tell us when a corporation may engage in electioneering that some of its shareholders oppose. It does not even resolve the specific question whether Citizens United may be required to finance some of its messages with the money in its PAC. The conceit that corporations must be treated identically to natural persons in the political sphere is not only inaccurate but also inadequate to justify the Court's disposition of this case. . . .

"The Court's ruling threatens to undermine the integrity of elected institutions across the Nation. The path it has taken to reach its outcome will, I fear, do damage to this institution. . . .

"In a democratic society, the longstanding consensus on the need to limit corporate campaign spending should outweigh the wooden application of judge-made rules. The majority's rejection of this principle 'elevate[s] corporations to a level of deference which has not been seen at least since the days when substantive due process was regularly used to invalidate regulatory legislation thought to unfairly impinge upon established economic interests.' At bottom, the Court's opinion is thus a rejection of the common sense of the American people, who have recognized a need to prevent corporations from undermining self-government since the founding, and who have fought against the distinctive corrupting potential of corporate electioneering since the days of Theodore Roosevelt. It is a strange time to repudiate that common sense. While American democracy is imperfect, few outside the majority of this Court would have thought its flaws included a dearth of corporate money in politics."

PARTIAL CONCURRING AND DISSENTING OPINION BY JUSTICE CLARENCE THOMAS

"Political speech is entitled to robust protection under the First Amendment. Section 203 of the Bipartisan Campaign Reform Act of 2002 (BCRA) has never been reconcilable with that protection. By striking down §203, the Court takes an important first step toward restoring full constitutional protection to speech that is 'indispensable to the effective and intelligent use of the processes of popular government.' I dissent from Part IV of the Court's opinion, however, because the Court's constitutional analysis does not go far enough. The disclosure, disclaimer, and reporting requirements in BCRA §§201 and 311 are also unconstitutional."

★　★　★

NATIONAL FEDERATION OF INDEPENDENT BUSINESS v. SEBELIUS

– 2012 –

By a narrow vote the Supreme Court upheld most, but not all, of the Affordable Care Act, the most expansive domestic legislation enacted in decades, aimed at expanding access to health care for millions of people.

The elusive goal of many presidents dating back to Theodore Roosevelt has been to expand health-care coverage to as many Americans as possible. Their proposals, with varying degrees of participation by employers, workers, and the government, failed—with the exception of the enactment of Medicare and Medicaid in 1965, which helped the elderly and disadvantaged obtain health care.

But President Barack Obama was determined to make health-care improvements the hallmark of his presidency. He was barely able to push through Congress the Patient Protection and Affordable Care Act in 2010—a nine-hundred-page, hastily drafted, and flawed statute that drew legal challenges as soon as it was signed into law. Among other things, it required private insurance providers to cover pre-existing conditions and allowed those without insurance to obtain it through state and federal exchanges.

But two provisions became the focal point of the constitutional challenge to the law. The first was the so-called "individual mandate" that required most Americans to obtain some kind of health insurance or face a penalty. The concept had been embraced by Republicans earlier in the debate over expanding health care as a way to help insurance companies afford broad coverage. But as soon as it became part of Obama's legislation, conservatives turned on the idea, portraying it as a "big government" intrusion on the right of individuals to decide whether or not to obtain coverage.

The other provision at issue encouraged states to expand their Medicaid programs for poor residents by penalizing the states with a big cut in subsidies if they did not. To many governors, this was a form of coercion that violated the sovereignty of the states.

As lower courts began ruling on these issues in cases brought by individuals, states, businesses, and employers, it became clear that the Supreme Court would be the ultimate referee to decide the fate of the largest new domestic program enacted by Congress in decades.

Because of the complexity of the cases before it, the court scheduled six hours of oral argument over three days, compared to the hour-long argument—a half hour for each side—that is allotted for almost all other cases, big or small.

Perhaps because of the length of the deliberations, one argument made by U.S. Solicitor General Donald Verrilli Jr. nearly escaped notice. He told the court that if it did not think the individual mandate could be justified as a congressional exercise of power over interstate commerce, it could be vindicated under the taxing power of Congress—in part because those who did not buy health insurance would have to pay their penalty as part of their annual income taxes.

That little-noticed argument carried the day for the Affordable Care Act. Chief Justice John Roberts Jr. wrote the opinion for the 5–4 court, announcing first that a majority of justices found that the individual mandate requirement was not a valid use of the commerce power. That led some media organizations to report that the Affordable Care Act had been struck down. But those reports were withdrawn after Roberts announced the second finding—that the mandate was a proper exercise of the taxing power, even though the legislation did not call it a tax.

As for the Medicaid issue, seven justices agreed that the law was coercive and infringed on states' prerogatives. That part of the decision threatened to undermine the economic model for the Affordable Care Act, but four years later the program was still running, despite repeated efforts by congressional Republicans to overturn the landmark legislation.

DECISION OF THE COURT
BY CHIEF JUSTICE JOHN ROBERTS JR.

"Today we resolve constitutional challenges to two provisions of the Patient Protection and Affordable Care Act of 2010: the individual mandate, which requires individuals to purchase a health insurance policy providing a minimum level of coverage; and the Medicaid expansion, which gives funds to the States on the condition that they provide specified health care to all citizens whose income falls below a certain threshold. We do not consider whether the Act embodies sound policies. That judgment is entrusted to the Nation's elected leaders. We ask only whether Congress has the power under the Constitution to enact the challenged provisions. . . .

"This case concerns two powers that the Constitution does grant the Federal Government, but which must be read carefully to avoid creating a general federal authority akin to the police power. The Constitution authorizes Congress to 'regulate Commerce with foreign Nations, and among the several States, and with the Indian Tribes.' Our precedents read that to mean that Congress may regulate 'the channels of interstate commerce,' 'persons or things in interstate commerce,' and 'those activities that substantially affect interstate commerce'. . . .

"Congress may also 'lay and collect Taxes, Duties, Imposts and Excises, to pay the Debts and provide for the common Defence and general Welfare of the United States.' Put simply, Congress may tax and spend. This grant gives the Federal Government considerable influence even in areas where it cannot directly regulate. The Federal Government may enact a tax on an activity that it cannot authorize, forbid, or otherwise control. . . .

"The Government contends that the individual mandate is within Congress's power because the failure to purchase insurance 'has a substantial and deleterious effect on interstate commerce' by creating the cost-shifting problem. . . .

"Given its expansive scope, it is no surprise that Congress has employed the commerce power in a wide variety of ways to address the pressing needs of the time. But Congress has never attempted to rely on that power to compel individuals not engaged in commerce to purchase an unwanted product. Legislative novelty is not necessarily fatal; there is a first time for everything. But sometimes 'the most telling indication of [a] severe constitutional problem . . . is the lack of historical precedent' for Congress's action. . . .

"Construing the Commerce Clause to permit Congress to regulate individuals precisely because they are doing nothing would open a new and potentially vast domain to congressional authority. Every day individuals do not do an infinite number of things. In some cases they decide not to do something; in others they simply fail to do it. Allowing

Congress to justify federal regulation by pointing to the effect of inaction on commerce would bring countless decisions an individual could potentially make within the scope of federal regulation, and— under the Government's theory—empower Congress to make those decisions for him. . . .

". . . The Framers gave Congress the power to regulate commerce, not to compel it, and for over 200 years both our decisions and Congress's actions have reflected this understanding. There is no reason to depart from that understanding now. . . .

"That is not the end of the matter. Because the Commerce Clause does not support the individual mandate, it is necessary to turn to the Government's second argument: that the mandate may be upheld as within Congress's enumerated power to 'lay and collect Taxes.'

"The Government's tax power argument asks us to view the statute differently than we did in considering its commerce power theory. In making its Commerce Clause argument, the Government defended the mandate as a regulation requiring individuals to purchase health insurance. The Government does not claim that the taxing power allows Congress to issue such a command. Instead, the Government asks us to read the mandate not as ordering individuals to buy insurance, but rather as imposing a tax on those who do not buy that product.

"The text of a statute can sometimes have more than one possible meaning. To take a familiar example, a law that reads 'no vehicles in the park' might, or might not, ban bicycles in the park. And it is well established that if a statute has two possible meanings, one of which violates the Constitution, courts should adopt the meaning that does not do so. . . .

"The States also contend that the Medicaid expansion exceeds Congress's authority under the Spending Clause. They claim that Congress is coercing the States to adopt the changes it wants by threatening to withhold all of a State's Medicaid grants, unless the State accepts the new expanded funding and complies with the conditions that come with it. This, they argue, violates the basic principle that the 'Federal Government may not compel the States to enact or administer a federal regulatory program.'

"In this case, the financial 'inducement' Congress has chosen is much more than 'relatively mild encouragement'—it is a gun to the head. Section 1396c of the Medicaid Act provides that if a State's Medicaid plan does not comply with the Act's requirements, the Secretary of Health and Human Services may declare that 'further payments will not be made to the State.' A State that opts out of the Affordable Care Act's expansion in health care coverage thus stands to lose not merely 'a relatively small percentage' of its existing Medicaid funding, but all of it. Medicaid spending accounts for over 20 percent of the average State's total budget, with federal funds covering 50 to 83 percent of those costs."

CONCURRING OPINION
BY JUSTICE RUTH BADER GINSBURG

"The provision of health care is today a concern of national dimension, just as the provision of old-age and survivors' benefits was in the 1930's. In the Social Security Act, Congress installed a federal system to provide monthly benefits to retired wage earners and, eventually, to their survivors. Beyond question, Congress could have adopted a similar scheme for health care. Congress chose, instead, to preserve a central role for private insurers and state governments. According to the Chief Justice, the Commerce Clause does not permit that preservation. This rigid reading of the Clause makes scant sense and is stunningly retrogressive. . . .

"In enacting the Patient Protection and Affordable Care Act (ACA), Congress comprehensively reformed the national market for health-care products and services. By any measure, that market is immense. Collectively, Americans spent $2.5 trillion on health care in 2009, accounting for 17.6% of our Nation's economy. Within the next decade, it is anticipated, spending on health care will nearly double. . . .

"Health-care providers do not absorb these bad debts. Instead, they raise their prices, passing along the cost of uncompensated care to those who do pay reliably: the government and private insurance companies. In response, private insurers increase their premiums, shifting the cost of the elevated bills from providers onto those who carry insurance. The net result: Those with health insurance subsidize the medical care of those without it. As economists would describe what happens, the uninsured "free ride" on those who pay for health insurance. . . .

"In sum, Congress passed the minimum coverage provision as a key component of the ACA to address an economic and social problem that has plagued the Nation for decades: the large number of U.S. residents who are unable or unwilling to obtain health insurance. Whatever one thinks of the policy decision Congress made, it was Congress' prerogative to make it. . . .

"Medicaid, as amended by the ACA, however, is not two spending programs; it is a single program with a constant aim—to enable poor persons to receive basic health care when they need it. Given past expansions, plus express statutory warning that Congress may change the requirements participating States must meet, there can be no tenable claim that the ACA fails for lack of notice. Moreover, States have no entitlement to receive any Medicaid funds; they enjoy only the opportunity to accept funds on Congress' terms."

DISSENTING OPINION BY JUSTICE ANTONIN SCALIA

"Congress has set out to remedy the problem that the best health care is beyond the reach of many Americans who cannot afford it. It can assuredly do that, by exercising the powers accorded to it under the Constitution. The question in this case, however, is whether the complex structures and provisions of the Patient Protection and Affordable Care Act (Affordable Care Act or ACA) go beyond those powers. We conclude that they do. . . .

". . . What is absolutely clear, affirmed by the text of the 1789 Constitution, by the Tenth Amendment ratified in 1791, and by innumerable cases of ours in the 220 years since, is that there are structural limits upon federal power—upon what it can prescribe with respect to private conduct, and upon what it can impose upon the sovereign States. Whatever may be the conceptual limits upon the Commerce Clause and upon the power to tax and spend, they cannot be such as will enable the Federal Government to regulate all private conduct and to compel the States to function as administrators of federal programs.

"That clear principle carries the day here. The striking case of *Wickard v. Filburn*, which held that the economic activity of growing wheat, even for one's own consumption, affected commerce sufficiently that it could be regulated, always has been regarded as the ne plus ultra of expansive Commerce Clause jurisprudence. To go beyond that, and to say the failure to grow wheat (which is not an economic activity, or any activity at all) nonetheless affects commerce and therefore can be federally regulated, is to make mere breathing in and out the basis for federal prescription and to extend federal power to virtually all human activity. . . .

"The Act before us here exceeds federal power both in mandating the purchase of health insurance and in denying nonconsenting States all Medicaid funding. These parts of the Act are central to its

design and operation, and all the Act's other provisions would not have been enacted without them.
In our view it must follow that the entire statute is
inoperative."

DISSENTING OPINION
BY JUSTICE CLARENCE THOMAS

"I dissent for the reasons stated in our joint opinion, but I write separately to say a word about the
Commerce Clause. The joint dissent and the Chief
Justice correctly apply our precedents to conclude
that the Individual Mandate is beyond the power
granted to Congress under the Commerce Clause
and the Necessary and Proper Clause. Under those
precedents, Congress may regulate 'economic
activity [that] substantially affects interstate commerce.' I adhere to my view that 'the very notion
of a "substantial effects" test under the Commerce
Clause is inconsistent with the original understanding of Congress' powers and with this Court's
early Commerce Clause cases.' As I have explained,
the Court's continued use of that test 'has encouraged the Federal Government to persist in its view
that the Commerce Clause has virtually no limits.'
The Government's unprecedented claim in this suit
that it may regulate not only economic activity but
also inactivity that substantially affects interstate
commerce is a case in point."

★　★　★

OBERGEFELL v. HODGES

– 2015 –

 ★   SAME-SEX MARRIAGE   ★

In a historic 5–4 ruling, the Supreme Court declared that same-sex couples are entitled to the right to marry under the Due Process and Equal Protection clauses of the Fourteenth Amendment.

The Supreme Court's momentum in the last half of the twentieth century was in the direction of expanding constitutional rights for racial and other minorities and women. But the court was slower to extend those rights to homosexuals, reflecting the public's lingering ambivalence toward gays and lesbians.

In 1986, the court in *Bowers v. Hardwick* upheld laws that made homosexual acts a crime. The ruling hampered progress that otherwise might have been made in expanding gay rights through litigation in the courts.

But at the beginning of the twenty-first century, the court shifted. In the 2003 case *Lawrence v. Texas*, a majority of the court decided that *Bowers* should be overturned. The court "misapprehended the claim of liberty" advanced in *Bowers*, the majority stated, and demeaned the dignity of gay Americans.

Obstacles to full equality remained, however. The federal Defense of Marriage Act, which defined marriage as between a man and a woman, was still in effect, depriving same-sex couples of a range of federal benefits even as some states began to recognize same-sex relationships. In the *United States v. Windsor* decision of 2013, that obstacle fell too, as the court ruled that the federal law interfered with "equal liberty."

In an angry dissent, Justice Antonin Scalia called the *Windsor* decision "argle-bargle" and asserted that it would provide a blueprint for future litigation against state bans on same-sex marriage. That prediction, to Scalia's regret, proved true.

Though some were worried that the high court might not be ready to fully embrace same-sex marriage, lawsuits from Michigan, Ohio, Kentucky, and Tennessee inexorably made their way to the Supreme Court. Most same-sex marriage advocates said there was no reason to wait. Most of the lower courts ruled in favor of recognizing same-sex marriage. When the U.S. Court of Appeals for the Sixth Circuit upheld Ohio's ban on same-sex marriages, the stage was set for the Supreme Court to take on the issue: The main reason the Supreme Court decides to review a case is to harmonize conflicting opinions in the courts below.

The cases the court agreed to hear were consolidated under the name of one of the cases, *Obergefell v. Hodges*. James Obergefell and his ailing partner John Arthur, both Ohio residents, married in Maryland in 2011, where such marriages were allowed, so that when Arthur died, Obergefell would be listed as his surviving spouse. That was not permitted under Ohio law, so Obergefell sued. Richard Hodges was director of the Ohio Department of Health.

As with the other major Supreme Court decisions that advanced gay rights, Justice Anthony Kennedy wrote the majority opinion. Joined by the liberal justices, Kennedy asserted that there was no valid reason to exclude gays from exercising the right to marry or to allow states the option of not recognizing such marriages performed in other states. Justices Ruth Bader Ginsburg, Stephen Breyer, Sonia Sotomayor, and Elena Kagan joined the majority.

The four conservatives—Chief Justice John Roberts Jr., Antonin Scalia, Clarence Thomas, and Samuel Alito Jr.—dissented, mainly citing the tradition that states set the rules for marriage, not the federal government, and that a change as significant as the one under consideration should be made through the political process, not by judges.

DECISION OF THE COURT
BY JUSTICE ANTHONY KENNEDY

"The Constitution promises liberty to all within its reach, a liberty that includes certain specific rights that allow persons, within a lawful realm, to define and express their identity. The petitioners in these cases seek to find that liberty by marrying someone of the same sex and having their marriages deemed lawful on the same terms and conditions as marriages between persons of the opposite sex. . . .

"From their beginning to their most recent page, the annals of human history reveal the transcendent importance of marriage. The lifelong union of a man and a woman always has promised nobility and dignity to all persons, without regard to their station in life. . . .

"That history is the beginning of these cases. The respondents say it should be the end as well. To them, it would demean a timeless institution if the concept and lawful status of marriage were extended to two persons of the same sex. Marriage, in their view, is by its nature a gender-differentiated union of man and woman. This view long has been held—and continues to be held—in good faith by reasonable and sincere people here and throughout the world.

"The petitioners acknowledge this history but contend that these cases cannot end there. Were their intent to demean the revered idea and reality of marriage, the petitioners' claims would be of a different order. But that is neither their purpose nor their submission. To the contrary, it is the enduring importance of marriage that underlies the petitioners' contentions. This, they say, is their whole point. . . .

"These new insights have strengthened, not weakened, the institution of marriage. Indeed, changed understandings of marriage are character- istic of a Nation where new dimensions of freedom become apparent to new generations, often through perspectives that begin in pleas or protests and then are considered in the political sphere and the judi- cial process. . . .

"This dynamic can be seen in the Nation's expe- riences with the rights of gays and lesbians. Until the mid-20th century, same-sex intimacy long had been condemned as immoral by the state itself in most Western nations, a belief often embodied in the criminal law. For this reason, among others, many persons did not deem homosexuals to have dignity in their own distinct identity. A truthful declaration by same-sex couples of what was in their hearts had to remain unspoken.

"Under the Due Process Clause of the Four- teenth Amendment, no State shall "deprive any person of life, liberty, or property, without due pro- cess of law." The fundamental liberties protected by this Clause include most of the rights enumerated in the Bill of Rights. In addition these liberties extend to certain personal choices central to indi- vidual dignity and autonomy, including intimate choices that define personal identity and beliefs.

"The nature of injustice is that we may not always see it in our own times. The generations that wrote and ratified the Bill of Rights and the Fourteenth Amendment did not presume to know the extent of freedom in all of its dimensions, and so they entrusted to future generations a charter protecting the right of all persons to enjoy liberty as we learn its meaning. When new insight reveals discord between the Constitution's central protections and a received legal stricture, a claim to liberty must be addressed. . . .

". . . [S]ame-sex couples are denied the constellation of benefits that the States have linked to marriage. This harm results in more than just material burdens. Same-sex couples are consigned to an instability many opposite-sex couples would deem intolerable in their own lives. As the State itself makes marriage all the more precious by the significance it attaches to it, exclusion from that status has the effect of teaching that gays and lesbians are unequal in important respects. It demeans gays and lesbians for the State to lock them out of a central institution of the Nation's society. Same-sex couples, too, may aspire to the transcendent purposes of marriage and seek fulfillment in its highest meaning. . . .

"The right to marry is fundamental as a matter of history and tradition, but rights come not from ancient sources alone. They rise, too, from a better informed understanding of how constitutional imperatives define a liberty that remains urgent in our own era. Many who deem same-sex marriage to be wrong reach that conclusion based on decent and honorable religious or philosophical premises, and neither they nor their beliefs are disparaged here. But when that sincere, personal opposition becomes enacted law and public policy, the necessary consequence is to put the imprimatur of the State itself on an exclusion that soon demeans or stigmatizes those whose own liberty is then denied. Under the Constitution, same-sex couples seek in marriage the same legal treatment as opposite-sex couples, and it would disparage their choices and diminish their personhood to deny them this right. . . .

"There may be an initial inclination in these cases to proceed with caution—to await further legislation, litigation, and debate. The respondents warn there has been insufficient democratic discourse before deciding an issue so basic as the definition of marriage. . . .

"The dynamic of our constitutional system is that individuals need not await legislative action before asserting a fundamental right. The Nation's courts are open to injured individuals who come to them to vindicate their own direct, personal stake in our basic charter. An individual can invoke a right to constitutional protection when he or she is harmed, even if the broader public disagrees and even if the legislature refuses to act. . . .

"No union is more profound than marriage, for it embodies the highest ideals of love, fidelity, devotion, sacrifice, and family. In forming a marital union, two people become something greater than once they were. As some of the petitioners in these cases demonstrate, marriage embodies a love that may endure even past death. It would misunderstand these men and women to say they disrespect the idea of marriage. Their plea is that they do respect it, respect it so deeply that they seek to find its fulfillment for themselves. Their hope is not to be condemned to live in loneliness, excluded from one of civilization's oldest institutions. They ask for equal dignity in the eyes of the law. The Constitution grants them that right."

DISSENTING OPINION
BY CHIEF JUSTICE JOHN ROBERTS JR.

"Petitioners make strong arguments rooted in social policy and considerations of fairness. They contend that same-sex couples should be allowed to affirm their love and commitment through marriage, just like opposite-sex couples. That position has undeniable appeal; over the past six years, voters and legislators in eleven States and the District of Columbia have revised their laws to allow marriage between two people of the same sex.

"But this Court is not a legislature. Whether same-sex marriage is a good idea should be of no concern to us. Under the Constitution, judges have power to say what the law is, not what it should be. The people who ratified the Constitution authorized courts to exercise 'neither force nor will but merely judgment.'

"Although the policy arguments for extending marriage to same-sex couples may be compelling, the legal arguments for requiring such an extension are not. The fundamental right to marry does not include a right to make a State change its definition of marriage. And a State's decision to maintain the meaning of marriage that has persisted in every culture throughout human history can hardly be called irrational. In short, our Constitution does not enact any one theory of marriage. The people of a State are free to expand marriage to include same-sex couples, or to retain the historic definition.

"Today, however, the Court takes the extraordinary step of ordering every State to license and recognize same-sex marriage. Many people will rejoice at this decision, and I begrudge none their celebration. But for those who believe in a government of laws, not of men, the majority's approach is deeply disheartening. Supporters of same-sex marriage have achieved considerable success persuading their fellow citizens—through the democratic process—to adopt their view. That ends today. Five lawyers have closed the debate and enacted their own vision of marriage as a matter of constitutional law. Stealing this issue from the people will for many cast a cloud over same-sex marriage, making a dramatic social change that much more difficult to accept. . . .

"The Court's accumulation of power does not occur in a vacuum. It comes at the expense of the people. And they know it. Here and abroad, people are in the midst of a serious and thoughtful public debate on the issue of same-sex marriage. They see voters carefully considering same-sex marriage, casting ballots in favor or opposed, and sometimes changing their minds. . . .

"But today the Court puts a stop to all that. By deciding this question under the Constitution, the Court removes it from the realm of democratic decision. There will be consequences to shutting down the political process on an issue of such profound public significance. Closing debate tends to close minds. People denied a voice are less likely to accept the ruling of a court on an issue that does not seem to be the sort of thing courts usually decide. . . .

"If you are among the many Americans—of whatever sexual orientation—who favor expanding same-sex marriage, by all means celebrate today's decision. Celebrate the achievement of a desired goal. Celebrate the opportunity for a new expression of commitment to a partner. Celebrate the availability of new benefits. But do not celebrate the Constitution. It had nothing to do with it."

DISSENTING OPINION BY JUSTICE ANTONIN SCALIA

"I write separately to call attention to this Court's threat to American democracy.

"The substance of today's decree is not of immense personal importance to me. The law can recognize as marriage whatever sexual attachments and living arrangements it wishes, and can accord them favorable civil consequences, from tax treatment to rights of inheritance. Those civil consequences—and the public approval that conferring the name of marriage evidences—can perhaps have adverse social effects, but no more adverse than the effects of many other controversial laws. So it is not of special importance to me what the law says about marriage. It is of overwhelming importance, however, who it is that rules me. Today's decree says that my Ruler, and the Ruler of 320 million Americans coast-to-coast, is a majority of the nine lawyers on the Supreme Court. The opinion in these cases is the furthest extension in fact—and the furthest extension one can even imagine—of the Court's claimed power to create "liberties" that the Constitution and its Amendments neglect to mention. This practice of constitutional revision by an unelected committee of nine, always accompanied (as it is today) by extravagant praise of liberty, robs the People of the most important liberty they asserted in the Declaration of Independence and won in the Revolution of 1776: the freedom to govern themselves.

"Until the courts put a stop to it, public debate over same-sex marriage displayed American democracy at its best. Individuals on both sides of the issue passionately, but respectfully, attempted to persuade their fellow citizens to accept their views. Americans considered the arguments and put the question to a vote. The electorates of 11 States, either directly or through their representatives, chose to expand the traditional definition of marriage. Many more decided not to. Win or lose, advocates for both sides continued pressing their cases, secure in the knowledge that an electoral loss can be negated by a later electoral win. That is exactly how our system of government is supposed to work."

DISSENTING OPINION
BY JUSTICE CLARENCE THOMAS

"The Court's decision today is at odds not only with the Constitution, but with the principles upon which our Nation was built. Since well before 1787, liberty has been understood as freedom from government action, not entitlement to government benefits. The Framers created our Constitution to preserve that understanding of liberty. Yet the majority invokes our Constitution in the name of a 'liberty' that the Framers would not have recognized, to the detriment of the liberty they sought to protect. Along the way, it rejects the idea—captured in our Declaration of Independence—that human dignity is innate and suggests instead that it comes from the Government. This distortion of our Constitution not only ignores the text, it inverts the relationship between the individual and the state in our Republic. I cannot agree with it."

DISSENTING OPINION
BY JUSTICE SAMUEL ALITO JR.

"Until the federal courts intervened, the American people were engaged in a debate about whether their States should recognize same-sex marriage. The question in these cases, however, is not what

States should do about same-sex marriage but whether the Constitution answers that question for them. It does not. The Constitution leaves that question to be decided by the people of each State.

"The Constitution says nothing about a right to same-sex marriage, but the Court holds that the term 'liberty' in the Due Process Clause of the Fourteenth Amendment encompasses this right. Our Nation was founded upon the principle that every person has the unalienable right to liberty, but liberty is a term of many meanings. For classical liberals, it may include economic rights now limited by government regulation. For social democrats, it may include the right to a variety of government benefits. For today's majority, it has a distinctively postmodern meaning.

"To prevent five unelected Justices from imposing their personal vision of liberty upon the American people, the Court has held that 'liberty' under the Due Process Clause should be understood to protect only those rights that are 'deeply rooted in this Nation's history and tradition.'"

★ ★ ★

ABOUT THE AUTHOR

Tony Mauro has covered the U.S. Supreme Court as a journalist since 1979, first for Gannett News Service and *USA Today*, and since 2000 for American Lawyer Media and *The National Law Journal*. A native of New York City, he received an undergraduate degree in political science from Rutgers University and a master's degree from Columbia University Graduate School of Journalism.

Washingtonian magazine has twice included Mauro on its list of the top fifty journalists in Washington. He is a longtime member of the steering committee of the Reporters Committee for Freedom of the Press, and in 2011 was inducted into the Freedom of Information Act Hall of Fame in recognition of his advocacy for openness in courts and other government institutions.

Mauro is the author of numerous law review articles and book chapters, as well as two books: *Illustrated Great Decisions of the Supreme Court*, published by CQ Press in 2006, and *Landmark Cases*, published in 2015 by C-SPAN and SAGE Publications/CQ Press.